The Thrifty London Guide
Volume 1

See More, Do More, Spend Less...

ISBN: - 13: 978-1492171386
ISBN: - 10: 1492171387

Cover Design by Louise Collarbon
www.designlc.co.uk

Inspiration
Steve Lowy
Umi Hotel London
www.umihotellondon.co.uk

Dedication:

This book is dedicated to my big brother Alan a true knowledgeable Londoner. Love you and miss you forever x

Contents

**Each section is filled with
Interesting Facts & Thrifty Tips**

*** Our Favourite Attractions for Family
visits are marked with an asterix**

Section 1
Out & About in London

Out & About in London

Travel Tips

Barclays Cycle Hire (Boris Bikes)
All Over London

Renting a bike in London is so easy with many docking stations dotted around the capital. Barclays Cycle Hire is the easiest way to get on a bike quickly. It's great if you want to hire a bike for a short time and is available to everyone over 14-years-old. Great fun and bikes cost as little as £1 for 24 hours.
See website for full details.
www.tfl.gov.uk/roadusers/cycling

Dr Bike
FREE Maintenance Clinics
London

If using your own bike in London Dr Bike cycle clinics are available on the 2nd and last Friday of every month to carry out FREE roadworthy checks and repairs.
www.cityoflondon.gov.uk

Remember Children under 5 travel FREE on all London Transport.

Oyster Card

A London Oyster card is the fastest, smartest and cheapest way to pay for single journeys on the bus, tube, DLR and London Overground, and Thames Clippers.

To find out how you can save visit the Oyster Card website:
www.oyster.tfl.gov.uk

London Buses
Many London buses pass by many of the sights and landmarks; these include Number 9, 11, 15 and 23.

Routemaster Bus No 9
Travels from Aldwych to Hammersmith, via Trafalgar Sq, Mayfair & Knightsbridge every 15 minutes

Routemaster Bus No 15
Travels from Poplar to Mayfair via St Paul's, Aldwych and Trafalgar Square, every 15 minutes

Routemaster Bus No 23
Passes St Pauls, Bank of England, Leicester Square, Soho, Covent Garden and more.
See the journey planner section of the Transport for London website for further details:
www.tfl.gov.uk

Interesting Fact
London Underground
London Underground (the Tube) was the first underground railway in the world.

Thrifty Tip
Tracey Emin Tube Map
Famous Artist Tracey Emin designed a tube map cover for London Underground in 2012 why not see if you can pick up a copy.
www.art.tfl.gov.uk

Crossing the Thames

* Thames River Bus
If you need to get somewhere quickly, why not jump on a boat. Most River Bus services provide a fast and frequent service from early morning until early evening - or later if there's an event at the O2 in North Greenwich.
Single fares start from £1.10p
www.tfl.gov.uk

The Woolwich Ferry River-Crossing
FREE Service
The Woolwich ferry is a FREE service operating between Woolwich and North Woolwich, linking the north and south circular roads across the Thames.
www.royalgreenwich.gov.uk

* Thames Cable Cars
Introducing the Emirates Air Line cable cars. Crossing the Thames to connect Greenwich Peninsula and the Royal Docks in just five minutes. The Emirates Air Line connects Emirates Royal Docks (North Terminal) and Emirates Greenwich Peninsula (South Terminal).

The Emirates Cable Cars have magnificent
Panoramic views of London.
Adult Single Fare £4.40 Child £2.20
www.emiratesairline.co.uk

Interesting Fact
Thames Cable Car
Emirates provide you with a map so you can
look out for your favourite Landmarks.

Thames Foot Tunnels

Greenwich Foot Tunnel
FREE
The Greenwich Foot Tunnel is a pedestrian
tunnel crossing beneath the River Thames,
linking Greenwich in the south with the Isle of
Dogs in the east.

Woolwich Foot Tunnel
FREE
Down river from Woolwich Ferry only a few
yards is Woolwich Foot Tunnel. The foot
tunnels at Greenwich and Woolwich are used
by 1.5m people a year and provide pedestrians
and cyclists with a safe way to cross the
Thames.
www.royalgreenwich.gov.uk/info/200102/w
alking/693/foot_tunnels

London Views

Buildings with Amazing Views of London

City Hall London SE1

City Hall is the headquarters of the Mayor of London and the London Assembly. It was designed by Norman Foster and opened in July 2002. At the top of the ten-story building is an exhibition and meeting space called London's Living Room it has an open viewing deck with views across the capital it is occasionally open to the public.

Admission FREE
www.london.gov.uk/city-hall

Interesting Fact
City Hall

The carpet covering the floor at City Hall is The London Photomat it is an aerial view of the whole of Greater London, at a detail precise enough to pinpoint individual houses and buildings.

Hays Gallery Hays Dock
London SE1

Hay's Galleria is a major riverside tourist attraction on the Jubilee Walk on the south bank of the River Thames. The Galleria's River Walkway has great views of the Thames, Tower Bridge the City and more.

Admission FREE
www.haysgalleria.co.uk

* Horniman Museum
London SE23

The Horniman Museum also has great views of London. If you visit don't miss the sundails in the Garden.

Admission FREE
www.horniman.ac.uk

London Sky Bar London SW1

Situated within Westminster's iconic Milbank Tower, The London Sky Bar offers panoramic views of the capital from four floors of London's tallest riverside building on the Thames.

www.londonskybar.com

* One New Change Roof Terrace
London EC4

At One New Change you can take in the spectacular views of St Paul's and the London skyline from the breathtaking public roof terrace, London's newest must see attraction.

www.onenewchange.com

* Royal Festival Hall London SE1

Although primarily a hall for major concerts, be sure to take the singing glass lift up to the fifth floor where you'll find a little-known balcony area with impressive views of the Thames.

Admission FREE
www.southbankcentre.co.uk

Royal Observatory
London SE10

The Royal Observatory Greenwich is on a hill and has a spectacular view of London.

Admission FREE
www.rmg.co.uk/royal-observatory

*Queen Elizabeth Hall
Southbank London SE1
The roof of Queen Elizabeth Hall has been
transformed into a beautiful roof garden.
The Roof Garden has fantastic panoramic views
to enjoy.
Admission FREE
www.southbankcentre.co.uk

*Thrifty Tip
Queen Elizabeth Hall Fountains
Jeppe Hein's "Appearing Rooms" fountain is
outside Queen Elizabeth Hall Southbank
Centre. The fountains are great fun for children
of all ages, a fantastic fun way to cool off on a
hot summer's day.

* Tate Modern Café London SE1
Tate Modern Café has excellent views of the
river Thames.
Admission FREE
www.tate.org.uk/visit/tate-modern

The Mounument London EC3
The Monument was built between 1671 and
1677 to commemorate the Great Fire of
London.

Designed by Sir Christopher Wren and Dr
Robert Hooke, It has become a place of historic
interest providing visitors with an opportunity
to look across London in all directions, from a
height of about 160 feet from the public gallery.

Admission Child: £1.50 Concessions £2.00
Adults £3.00
www.themonument.info

Interesting Fact
The Monument
The Monument is the tallest free standing stone
column in the world.

* Tower Bridge London SE1
The bridge was designed by Sir Horace Jones,
and is one of the most impressive bridges in the
world. Enjoy stunning views of London from
the high level walkways.
Admission Child £2.83 Concessions £4.67
Adults £6.67
www.towerbridge.org.uk

* Interesting Facts
Tower Bridge
Lift Times
Tower Bridge is lifted several times per week to
allow river traffic to pass under it. To see lifting
times see website:
www.towerbridge.org.uk

* Tower Bridge/
St Katharine's Dock
St Katherine's Dock is a vibrant Marina just
next to Tower Bridge it's a fantastic location.
It has shops, bars and restaurants and it a great
place to sit and watch boats arriving through the
historic dock.

The Dock holds various FREE events see
website for details:
www.skdocks.co.uk

* Wellington Arch Hyde Park
London W1
Wellington Arch was built in 1825-7 Intended
as a victory arch proclaiming Wellington's
defeat of Napoleon, it is crowned by the largest
bronze sculpture in Europe the Angel of Peace.
Visitors can enjoy the glorious panoramas over
London's Parks and the Houses of Parliament
from the balconies.
Admission only £3
www.english-heritage.org.uk

Interesting Fact
Wellington Arch
The Quadriga Gallery
In addition to a new exhibition about the
history of Wellington Arch, the London
landmark now houses an additional exhibition
space The Quadriga Gallery where a series of
exhibitions exploring the past, present and
future of England's heritage will be taking place.

* Thrifty Tip
Wellington Arch
Try to time your visit to Wellington Arch before
the Changing of the Guard ceremony.
Then you can view the Household Cavalry in
their red tunics and bearskin hats on their way
to and from the Changing of the Guard.

Thrifty Tip
Wellington Apsley House

(Number One London)
Wellington's family home was Apsley House one of the capital's finest Georgian buildings. The house is oposite Wellington Arch and can be visited.
Admission Concessions £5.90 Adults £6.50
www.english-heritage.org.uk

Interesting Fact
Napoleon
Napoleon was defeated under the command of the Duke of Wellington at the Battle of Watterloo.

Napoleon 111
Napoleon 111 home in London was 1c King Street SW1, he lived here whilst working in Chancery Lane London as a Lawyer.

Westminster Cathedral Bell Tower
London SE1
The Campanile Bell Tower, 273 ft in height, is dedicated to St Edward. The level is accessible by elevator and offers spectacular 360° views across London.
Admission Concessions: £2.50 (students and seniors) Adults £5.00.
www.Westminstercathedral.org.uk

Other London Views

* Thames Cable Car
The Emirates Cable Cars have magnificent Panoramic views of London.
Adult Single Fare £4.40 Child £2.20
www.emiratesairline.co.uk

Interesting Fact
Thames Cable Car
Emirates provide you with a map so you can
look for your favourite Landmarks.

* Millennium Bridge London
When walking from south to north on the
Millennium Bridge you can see great views of St
Paul's Cathedral.

Parks & Heaths with Amazing Views of London

Amazing panoramic views of London can also
be seen from the following Parks & Heaths:
Alexandra Palace, Greenwich Park (which has a
viewing platform) Parliament Hill and Primrose
Hill.

* Island Gardens
London E14
Noted for its spectacular cross-river view of the
classical buildings of the former Greenwich
Hospital the National Maritime Museum and
the beautiful Greenwich Park.
www.towerhamlets.gov.uk

* Wimbledon Lawn Tennis Club
London SW19
Wimbledon has an amazing view of London
from the famous Hill (AKA Henman Hill).
www.wimbledon.com

Ceremonies & Royal Parades

* Ceremony of the Keys
Tower of London EC3
The Ceremony of the Keys is the traditional locking up of the Tower of London and has taken place each night, without fail, for at least 700 years.
Admission FREE
Apply in writing see website.
www.hrp.org.uk

Interesting Fact
Ceremony of the Keys
The importance of securing this fortress for the night is still very relevant because, although the Monarch no longer resides at this royal palace, the Crown Jewels and many other valuables still do.

Thrifty Tip
Tower of London
If you live in Tower Hamlets you can visit the Tower for just £1.
www.hrp.org.uk

Changing the Guard

* Buckingham Palace London SW1
Changing The Guards
Buckingham Palace Foot Guards provide a colourful display in their red tunics and bearskins at the changing the guard ceremony.

The guards are accompanied by a band throughout the ceremony. It is held daily from May to July, at 11.30 and on alternate dates throughout the rest of the year see website: **www.royal.gov.uk/RoyalEventsandCeremonies**

Interesting Fact
Buckingham Palace
When the Royal Standard flag flies on the roof of Buckingham Palace the Queen is in residence.

Interesting Fact
The Queen
The Queen was born on 21 April 1926, her birthplace was 17 Bruton Street London W1. The young princess Elizabeth was the first child of The Duke and Duchess of York, who later became King George VI and Queen Elizabeth.

* Horse Guards Arch London W1
Changing the Guard
Changing the Guard takes place daily at 11.00am (10.00am on Sundays) and lasts about half an hour.

It is normally held on Horse Guards Parade by the arch of Horse Guards building see website: **www.royal.gov.uk/RoyalEventsandCeremonies**

Royal Parades

* Trooping the Colour
Horse Guards &
Buckingham Palace
London
The Sovereign's official birthday is celebrated by the ceremony of Trooping the Colour on a Saturday in June. The parade is carried out by fully trained and operational troops, and accompanied by marching bands and horses it is a true spectacle of English Pageantry.

The parade is attended by the Queen and other members of the Royal family. The parade ends with The Queen and members of the Royal family on the balcony at Buckingham Palace and an RAF fly past.
FREE Annual Event see website:
www.royal.gov.uk

English Heritage
Blue Plaques Scheme

London's English Heritage Blue Plaques scheme commemorates the link between notable figures of the past and the buildings in which they lived and worked.

The properties are FREE to view from the outside below is a small selection of the properties available to view:

Properties include that of Jane Austen Author, Isambard Kingdom Brunel Civil Engineer,

Charles Darwin, Charles Dickens, John Logie Baird inventor, Constable Artist/Painter, Karl Marx, Mozart, Sir Isaac Newton, Napoleon 111, George Orwell Author, Samuel Pepys Diarist, Shelley and many more.

To find an address of where a notable figure of the past lived or worked visit the English Heritage website:
www.english-heritage.org.uk/discover/blue-plaques/search

Interesting Fact
Charles Dickens &
The George and the Vulture
London EC3
Charles Dickens drank at The George and The Vulture pub, and it is mentioned at least 20 times in The Pickwick Papers by Charles Dickens.

Walking Tours

Tower Hill
FREE Walking Tour
Walking Tour leaves opposite tower hill tube daily 10am and 4pm.

Wellington Arch
FREE Walking Tour
Hyde Park Corner London W1
Every day leaving Wellington Arch at 11am and 3pm.
www.newlondon-tours.com/daily-tours/royal-london-free-tour.html

* Thames Path Nation Trail

Thames Path Walk is a beautiful walk that runs through the heart of London, along the River Thames. It is well signposted with the National Trail Symbol.

www.thames-path.org.uk

Section 2
Architecture & Design

Section 2
Architecture & Design

Architecture

Archkids
FREE Festival

Archikids Festival is Open-City's flagship architecture festival for families. The weekend event allows children, and their families, time to explore the architecture of the City of London's Square Mile by participating in the festival's inspiring architectural activities, tours and workshops.

FREE annual event see website for dates
www.opencity.org.uk

Open House Weekend
FREE EVENT

London has some amazing architecture including Art Deco, Baroque, Georgian, Gothic, Modern and more. Open House is your chance to explore hundreds of inspiring buildings in London FREE of charge. It's the biggest celebration of London's architecture.

Annual Event September
Admission FREE
www.londonopenhouse.org

The Thrifty London Guide's favourite pieces of London Architecture are listed below:

Art Deco

Battersea Power Station London SW8

A decommissioned Grade 11 listed power station built in the 1930's. Battersea was designed by a team of architects and civil engineers; the team was headed by Dr Leonard Pearce the chief engineer of the London Power Company.
www.batterseapowerstation.co.uk

Claridges Hotel London W1

Some of the world's greatest designers have left their mark on Claridge's. Original features mingle with distinctly modern twists, with the effortless Art Deco elegance that makes London's finest hotel a true Art Deco jewel.
www.claridges.co.uk

Interesting Fact
Claridges Hotel

During World War Two suite 212 at Claridges was declared Yugoslavian territory (At the request of Winston Churchill), so that Crown Prince Alexander II could be born on his own country's soil. He is still a regular visitor.

Florin Court
Smithfield EC1

An Art Deco residential building built in 1936 by Guy Morgan & Partners. Florin Court has a very impressive curved façade.

Interesting Fact
Florin Court and
Agatha Christie's Poirot
Florin Court was used by the BBC as the home
of Poirot (known as Poirot's Whitehaven
Mansions) for the drama series.

* Odeon Cinema Leicester Square WC2
Built in the 1930's by Weedon & Mather the
building has a magnificent Art Deco black
polished granite facade and high tower
displaying its name.

Interesting Fact
Odeon Leicester Square
The Odeon Leicester Square regularly plays host
to premieres and other red carpet events.
www.odeon.co.uk

Baroque

Christ Church Spitalfields
Hawksmoor's church is now recognised as one
of the high points of English baroque. Limited
opening see website for full details.
www.ccspitalfields.org

Thrifty Tip
Christ Church Spitalfields
FREE Concerts and Recitals See website for
listings.
www.ccspitalfields.org

Brutalist

Trelick Tower North Kensington
London W10

The tower was designed in the brutalist style by architect Erno Goldfinger for the GLC. The flats were originally built for social housing and is by far the most famous piece of social housing in London. However several of the flats are now privately owned.

Interesting Fact
Erno Goldfinger
2 Willow Road London NW3

This Modernist show home was designed by architect Ernő Goldfinger as a home for himself and his family, and was built in 1938. The house has surprising design details that were ground-breaking at the time and still feel fresh today.
Admission Concession £3 Adult £6
www.nationaltrust.org.uk

Georgian

Benjamin Franklin House

Each Monday Benjamin Franklin House offers Architectural tours about the history of Benjamin Franklin House with a guide.
The Georgian features of the 1730s building are revealed along with its fascinating history.
www.benjaminfranklinhouse.org

Gothic

Eton School Eton Berks

The School Yard lies at the heart of the ancient buildings. Other Buildings include the College Chapel a fine example of fifteenth century Perpendicular Gothic architecture.

Tour Concessions £6.50 Adults £7.50

Admission FREE for some see website for details

www.eton.com

Interesting Fact
Eton School

The wall paintings at Eton are among the most remarkable mediaeval wall paintings in Northern Europe, there are also remarkable stained glass windows.

Guildhall London EC2

The present Guildhall was begun in 1411 and, having survived both the Great Fire of London and the Blitz, it is the only secular stone structure dating from before 1666 still standing in the City. The grand gothic entrance was added by George Dance in 1788.

www.guildhall.cityoflondon.gov.uk

Interesting Fact
Guildhall

The Medievil crypts that lie beneath Guildhall are the largest medieval crypts in London.

* Houses of Parliament & Big Ben (Palace of Westminster) London W1

One of the most recognised buildings in the world the Palace of Westminster owes its stunning Gothic architecture to Sir Charles Barry, assisted by Austus Pugin an authority on Gothic architecture and style.

Interesting Fact
Houses of Parliament

The Palace is Grade I listed and part of an UNESCO World Heritage Site; it contains a mixture of both ancient and modern buildings, and houses an iconic collection of art.

Houses of Parliament
BIG BEN

Big Ben is the world's largest four-faced chiming turret clock it was designed by Pugin and is situated in the Elizabeth Tower. The clock is commonly known as 'Big Ben' but this phase actually only refers to the main bell housed within the Clock Tower.

Interesting Facts
Big Ben

In 2012 the Big Ben Bell Tower's name was changed from St Stephens Tower to Elizabeth Tower to honour the Queen's Diamond Jubilee.

Big Ben Chimes

The best time to visit the Palace of Westminster building is on the hour so you can hear live the wonderful chimes of "Big Ben".

Thrifty Tip
Big Ben
If you are a resident of the UK and you would like to visit Big Ben Clock Tower and see the Bell of Big Ben you can apply via your local MP.
www.parliament.uk

Thrifty Tip
Houses of Parliament
Parliament is open to all UK and overseas visitors to attend debates, watch committee hearings. Or you can take a tour inside one of the world's most iconic buildings.
www.parliament.uk

Medieval

The Jewel Tower London W1
An intriguing visitor attraction in the heart of Westminster that dates back almost 650 years. It was built around 1365 to house Edward III's treasures and was known as the 'King's Privy Wardrobe'.
Child 2.30 Concession £3.50 Adults £3.90
www.english-heritage.org.uk

Modern

City Hall London SE1
City Hall is located between London Bridge and Tower Bridge, on the south bank of the Thames.

The striking rounded glass building that is City Hall was designed by Norman Foster and Partners, one of Britain's leading architects www.morelondon.com

Interesting Fact
City Hall
City Hall has many features that make it environmentally friendly these include solar panels on the roof.

* City Hall Scoop Fountains London SE1
The fountains outside City Hall and the Scoop amphitheatre are lit beautifully and are continuous falling jets.

Container City 1 Trinity Buoy Wharf London Docklands
The original container city project is an innovative modular system that creates affordable accommodation (from Containers) for a range of uses.

Interesting Fact
Container City 1
Container City took just five months to complete in 2001.
www.containercity.com/home.html

Lloyds of London Lime Street EC3
Was designed by architect Richard Rogers and built between 1978 and 1986. Like the Pompidou Centre (designed by Renzo Piano and Rogers).

The building was innovative in having its services such as staircases, lifts, electrical power conduits and water pipes on the outside, leaving an uncluttered space inside.

Interesting Fact
Lutine Bell at Lloyds
The Lutine was a French Navy frigate, the British captured her and took her into the Royal Navy as HMS *Lutine,* and sadly she was lost in 1799. Lloyd's of London has preserved her bell. The Lutine bell was traditionally struck when news of an overdue ship arrived. Due to damage to the bell it is no longer rang.

Interesting Fact
Lloyds
Also at Lloyds displayed in a cabinet is Lloyds Nelson's collections including the orignal logbook of HMS Euralyus an observer at the battle of Trafalgar.
www.lloyds.com

30 St Mary Axe
(AKA The Gherkin)
London EC3
A Skyscrapper in London's financial district in the City completed in December 2003 and opened at the end of May 2004. The building was designed by Norman Foster and Arup engineers. This stunning glass tower is AKA the Gherkin because of its shape.
www.30stmaryaxe.com

The Orangery GOSH London WC1
Great Ormond Street Hospital wanted to create a conservatory style building for eating and drinking that offered visitors a tranquil escape. So Spacelab transformed an unused and unloved roof area into a striking sculptural pavilion in timber and glass.

Interesting Fact
Peter Pan
Great Ormond Street Hospital
Sir James Mathew Barrie (JM Barrie) novelist and playwright gave all the royalties from his famous children's book *Peter Pan* to Great Ormond Street Hospital for sick children.

* The Shard London Bridge SE1
The Shard is the tallest completed building in Europe has redefined London's Skyline. The tower has 72 floors, with a viewing gallery and open-air observation deck on the 72nd floor. The Shard was designed in 2000 by Renzo Piano the building is a magnificent piece of modern architecture.

Interesting Fact
The Shard
It is said the first designs of the building were written on a beer mat.
www.the-shard.com

Neo Classical

Kenwood House Hampstead
London NW3

This stunning neo classical house has beautiful gardens that include a lake and sculptors by Sir Henry Moore. The house is closed until autumn 2013 but the gardens and café are open.
Admission FREE
www.english-heritage.org.uk

Interesting Fact
Kenwood House
The house was used for part of the filming of Notting Hill with Hugh Grant & Julia Roberts.
www.english-heritage.org.uk

Tudor Style

Shakespeare's Globe Theatre London SE1

The Globe has a magnificent thatched roof, the first in London since the Great Fire.
Techniques used in the reconstruction of the Elizabethan playhouse of the circular theatre were painstakingly accurate.

Interesting Fact
Shakespeare's Globe Theatre
The project to rebuild Shakespeare's Globe was initiated by the American actor, director and producer Sam Wanamaker after his first visit to London in 1949.

Thrifty Tips
Shakespeare's Globe
Love Shakespeare's work?
Yard standing tickets are available for
performances at Shakespeare's Globe for just
£5. Yard standing is a wonderful experience and
it offers one of the best views of the stage.

Shakespeare's Globe
Tours of the Globe are available
see website for details:
www.shakespearesglobe.com

Unusual Architecture

Cheyne Walk London SW3
The Beautiful Riverside Mansions at Cheyne
Walk Chelsea are well worth a visit. Cheyne
Walk has had many famous residence including
Brunel, George Elliot, Mick Jagger, Kieth
Richards, and John Paul Getty 11.

Garrick's Temple Hampton
The temple has a beautiful spot on the Riverside
at Hampton was built by the great 18th century
actor-manager David Garrick in 1756 to
celebrate the genius of William Shakespeare.
The Temple is open to the public on Sunday
(14.00-17.00) from the first Sunday in April to
October.
Admission FREE unless otherwise stated
www.garrickstemple.org.uk

Neasden Temple London NW10

BAPS Shri Swaminarayan Mandir popularly known as the Neasden Temple, is the first traditional Hindu Mandir in Europe. The Temple is a masterpiece of exotic design. The stunning architectural masterpieces was created from the conceptual design and vision of His Holiness Pramukh Swami Maharaji, and the architect C. B. Sompura and his team.
www.mandir.org

Village Underground London EC2

High above Great Eastern Street on top of The Venue, four recycled Jubilee line train carriages and shipping containers make up the creative studios of Village Underground.

Thrifty Tip
Village Underground

Various Exhibitions and events take place at village underground many of which are
Admission FREE
www.villageunderground.co.uk

Interior Design

Astoria/Rainbow Finsbury Park London N5

The Astoria/Rainbow is a Grade 11 Listed building; the Interior is designed as a Moorish walled city, and has amazing atmospherics. The entrance hall has decorated columns, mosaic tiling, and a twinkling fountain.

The building designed by Stone & Somerford summonds up all the mystery and enchantment of a harem. The building is now a Pentacostal Church and it is well worth a visit
Tel: 0207 263 3385

2 Willow Road Hampstead London NW3
This Modernist show home was designed by architect Ernő Goldfinger as a home for himself and his family, and was built in 1938. The house has surprising design details that were ground-breaking at the time and still feel fresh today.
Admission Concession £3 Adult £6
www.nationaltrust.org.uk

All Hallows by the Tower London EC3
This church has many design treasures inside including beautiful font cover carved in Limewood by Grinling Gibbons. There is also a collection of medieval brasses.
www.allhallowsbythetower.org.uk

Banqueting House Ceiling Paintings London SW1
The ceiling paintings at Banqueting House are the most important commissions of their kind surviving in London. They were painted by one of the most important artists of the age, Sir Peter Paul Rubens.
www.hrp.org.uk/BanquetingHouse

* British Museum London WC1

The British Museum was designed in the nineteenth century. Smirke designed the building in the Greek revival style which emulated classical Greek architecture. Greek features on the building include the columns and pediment at the South entrance. The round Reading Room has a domed ceiling, and the stunning Norman Foster designed Glass Great Court opened in 2000.

www.britishmuseum.org

Buddhapadipa Temple London SW19

The walls are decked with a series of intricate paintings (murals) depicting the life of Buddha. These murals were the work of some sixteen artists who spent four years completing the task.

www.buddhapadipa.org

Interesting Fact
Buddhapadipa Temple
Buddhapadipa means 'The light of Wisdom'.

Chapter House Westminster Abbey London SW1

Chapter house has a very impressive medievil tiled floor – possibly the finest in England

www.Westminster-abbey.org

Interesting Fact
Chapter House
The origins of Parliament began at Chater House.

Christ Church Spitalfields London E1

Christ Church has a stunning organ by famous organ builder Richard Bridge. The organ was installed in the church in 1735 and is considered to be the masterpiece of the greatest organ builder in Georgian England.
www.christchurchspitalfields.org

Claridges Hotel London W1

Some of the world's greatest designers have left their mark on Claridge's Hotel, and it has one of the grandist Art Deco interiors in London. The huge sparkling Dale Chihuly light sculpture (A Million Pound Chandelier) can be viewed in the grand art deco setting of the Foyer.
www.claridges.co.uk

Eton School Berkshire

The wall paintings at Eton are among the most remarkable mediaeval wall paintings in Northern Europe, and the stained glass windows are remarkable.
Tour Prices Students and Concessions £6.50
Adults £7.50
Free entry for some see website:
www.etoncollege.com

* Guildhall London EC2

The imposing medieval hall at the Guildhall has stained glass windows and several monuments to national heroes including Admiral Lord Nelson, the Duke of Wellington and Sir Winston Churchill.
www.guildhall.cityoflondon.gov.uk

* Lambeth Palace Great Hall London SE1
Lambeth Palace Great Hall was designed by Christopher Wren it has arguably one of the greatest hammer beam roofs in London. For details of open days see website:
www.archbishopofcanterbury.org

Interesting Fact
Lambeth Palace
Lambeth Palace is the historic residence of the Archbishops of Canterbury. The Rt Revd Justin Welby is the present Archbishop of Canterbury.

Leighton House Holland Park Road London W14
The Arab Hall is its stunning centerpiece. Designed to display Leighton's priceless collection of over a thousand Islamic tiles, mostly brought back from Damascus in Syria. The interior evokes a compelling vision of the Orient.
Admission only £5
www.rbkc.gov.uk/subsites/museums/leigh tonhousemuseum.aspx

Masonic Temple at Andaz Hotel London Liverpool Street EC2
Andaz Hotel owned by the Hyatt chain has some amazing features, including the historic and beautiful Masonic Temple. The Temple has a Grade I listed interior status
www.london.liverpoolstreet.andaz.hyatt.co m

Methodist Central Hall London SW1
The domed ceiling of the Great Hall is reputed
to be the second largest of its type in the world.
The vast scale of the self-supporting ferro-
concrete structure reflects the original intention
that Central Hall was intended to be an open-air
meeting place with a roof on.
www.methodist-central-hall.org.uk

Interesting Fact
Methodist Central Hall Organ
William Lloyd Webber (father of Andrew &
Julian) was the Director of music at Central hall
he also played the organ there.

Thrifty Tip
Methodist Central Hall
Organ Concerts
The Organ at Cental Hall was originally build by
Arthur Hill in 1912, it was restored in 2011 by
Harrison & Harrison the organ has 4 Manuals
and 66 Stops. Organ concert events take place
at the church.
Admission £3
www.methodist-central-hall.org.uk

* Natural History Museum
Central Hall Ceiling London SW7
Natural History Museum has an art exhibition
that you could easily miss, its a wonderful
spread of ceiling panels decorated with plants
from every corner of the globe. Beautiful in
design, richly coloured and gilded, each with its
own story to tell.
Admission FREE
www.nhm.ac.uk

Neasden Temple London NW10

Neasden Temple is the first traditional Hindu Mandir in Europe, is a masterpiece of exotic design. The architectural masterpieces was created from the conceptual design and vision of His Holiness Pramukh Swami Maharaji, and the architect C. B. Sompura and his team.
www.mandir.org

Notre Dame De France London WC1

Has Murals by french artist and designer Jean Cocteau. There is a beautiful Aubusson tapestry behind the alter by Benedictine monk Dom Robert the well-known tapestry artist. There is also a mosaic of the Nativity by Boris Anrep the Russian artist and mosaic specialist.
www.ndfchurch.org

Interesting Fact
Boris Anrep

Russian artist and mosaic specialist Boris Anrep known for his mosaics in Westminster Cathedral, the National Gallery and the Bank of England.
www.ndfchurch.org

Old Royal Naval College Painted Hall Greenwich London SE10

The Painted Hall at ORNC is often described as the 'finest dining hall in Europe'. Designed by Sir Christopher Wren and Nicholas Hawksmoor. Its exuberant wall and ceiling decorations are by James Thornhill.
Admission FREE
www.ornc.org

Interesting Fact
Christopher Wren & Hawksmoor
Nicolas Hawksmoor was Wren's clerk and
pupil.
www.ornc.org

* Thrifty Tip
Greenwich FREE International Festival
Don't miss the Annual FREE Greenwich
International Festival with a line up of
International and UK Outdoor Arts, including
outdoor theatre, outdoor dance, and
installations see website for dates:
www.ornc.org/events/detail/greenwichdoc
klands-international-festival1

* Orleans House & Gallery
Twickenham TW1
The Baroque Octagon Room is a masterpiece
designed by James Gibbs in the early 18th
century. There are also 19th century Stables
buildings.
www.richmond.gov.uk/orleans_house_galle
ry

Royal Exchange London EC3
The giant murals were installed in 1892 around
the upper floor gallery of the central courtyard.
The impressive murals were painted by leading
artists of the day and illustrate the history of the
Royal Exchange and the City of London.
www.theroyalexchange.co.uk

Interesting Fact
Royal Exchange

Statue of George Peabody

At the Royal Exchange you can see a statue of the American philanthropist George Peabody. Peabody spent his fortune building homes for the poor of London, many of the homes known as "peabody Buildings" can still be seen in London today.

St Alfege's London SE10

There has been a church located here since the 11th century. Nicholas Hawksmoor designed the current building in 1714. It is an imposing Georgian structure featuring murals by James Thornhall, and beautiful stained glass windows. With carvings by master wood carver Grinling Gibbons.
www.st-alfege.org

Interesting Fact
Grinling Gibbons

Grinling Gibbons (1648-1721) was a sculptor and wood carver known for his work at St Paul's Cathedral, and Hampton Court Palace. Born and educated in Holland. Grinling Gibbons was once regarded as the finest wood carver in England.

St Bartholemews the Great Church
London EC1

The church has a rare and very beautiful oriel window that was built by Prior William Bolton.
www.greatstbarts.com

Interesting Fact
St Bartholemews the Great Church
The church was used in the filming of Four
Weddings and a Funeral and Shakespeare in
Love.

Thrifty Tip
St Bartholemews Museum
St Bartholemews has a small Museum which
contains William Hogarth's famous biblical
paintings. Tours take place every Friday see
website:
Tel: 0207 601 8152
**www.bartsandthelondon.nhs.uk/about-
us/museums**

St Brides Church Crypt London EC4
Archaeologists discovered that St Bride's stands
on Roman remains dating back to the 2nd
century A.D, including a Roman pavement.
Visitors interested in the church's Roman
origins can now enter the crypt to see the
original Roman ruins.
www.stbrides.com

Interesting Facts
St Brides Church
It is said that the spire of St Brides inspired the
designs for the British traditional tiered wedding
cake.

St Brides is known as the journalist's church
because of its links with Fleet Street.

Famous men and women of literature and history have links to St Brides church, the diarist Samuel Pepys and John Milton where both parishioners.

Thrifty Tip
St Brides Church
FREE lunchtime recitals
See website for full listings:
www.stbrides.com

St Magnus the Martyr
London EC3
Marvel at the beautiful interior.Also see their world-famous 4 metre long model of the old London Bridge. The church is built where all people crossing the old London Bridge used to enter the City. It has seen many important events in its 1000 year history.
www.stmagnusmartyr.org.uk

Interesting Facts
St Magnus the Martyr
The church has the first "Swell" organ in the UK it was built by Abraham Jordan in 1712.

Miles Coverdale
The church has a monument to Miles Coverdale (1487-1569) Coverdale was once Rector here. Coverdale oversaw the production of the first complete bible in English published in 1535.

Thrifty Tip
St Magnus the Martyr Bells
The bells are rung every Sunday by the Guild of St Magnus at 12:15. Visiting ringers are always made welcome.
www.stmagnusmartyr.org.uk

St Marys Woolnorth London SE16
The interior of this church is based on an Egyptian Hall is considered to be one of Hawksmoor's finest, there are also rich carvings by Grinling Gibbons.
www.stml.org.uk

Interesting Fact
St Marys Woolnorth
Christopher Jones Captain of The Mayflower is buried in the churchyard.

Interesting Fact
John Newton
John Newton once the rector at St Mary's wrote the hymn Amazing Grace.
http://stml.org.uk

St Mary Abbots Church
Kensington London W8
St Marys has two mosaics to either side of the reredos are memorials dated 1882, by Salviati from Venice. The sanctuary murals include a large wall painting in oils entitled "Feed my Sheep", showing the Risen Christ with 11 Apostles and with sheep grazing and resting.
www.smanews.weebly.com

Interesting Fact
St Mary Abbots Church
Healing Window
The Miracles of Healing Window was given by
the Royal College of Surgeons and others in
memory of Sir Isaac Newton.

Thrifty Tip
St Mary Abbots Church
Summer Fete
The St Mary Abbots Summer Fete is an annual
event, and is a fun day out for the entire family.
www.smanews.weebly.com

St Paul's Cathedral London EC4
Sir James Thornhill painted the eight stunning
paintings of the life of St Paul that line the
interior of the stunning dome. The man
responsible for the woodwork, including the
choir stalls is Grinling Gibbons. The beautiful
ceiling mosaics which are a must see are by
various artists including Alfred Stevens, George
Frederick Watts and William Blake.
www.stpauls.co.uk

Interesting Fact
St Paul's Cathedral
Great Paul is the bell of St Paul's it is the largest
Bell in Britain it is rung at 1pm daily

Thrifty Tip
St Paul's Cathedral
FREE Sunday Organ Recitals at
Sunday Organ Recitals take place weekly at
4.45pm.

These recitals are free and last about 30 minutes. All are welcome to attend.

St Stephens Walbrrok London EC4
Many consider this church to be Sir Christopher Wrens Masterpiece. The beauty of the interior draws you. Sir John Sommerson has described the Church as 'the pride of English architecture, and one of the few City churches in which the genius of Wren shines in full splendour'. Sir Nikolaus Pevsner lists it as one of the ten most important buildings in England.
www.ststephenwalbrook.net

Interesting Fact
St Stephens Walbrrok
Dr Chad Varah was once Rector of St Stephens and he founded the Samaratans from St Stephens in 1953.

Thrifty Tip
St Stephens Walbrook
FREE Organ Recitles & Concerts see website for full details.

The George Borough High Street London SE1
The George is London's only surviving galleried coaching inn. It stands on the south side of the River Thames near London Bridge. For centuries this was the only bridge across the river.
www.nationaltrust.org.uk/george-inn

The Lady Chapel Westminster Abbey
London SW1

The outstanding feature of the chapel is the spectacular fan-vaulted roof with its carved pendants. Around the walls are 95 statues of saints. Behind the altar is the tomb of Henry VII and his queen Elizabeth of York.
www.westminster-abbey.org

The Oak Room London EC1

The Metropolitan Water Board building is now luxury flats, however the buildings original oak panneled function room which was a work by woodcarver Grinling Gibbons remains intact. There are several public viewings throughout the year.
0207 883 9527

Trocadero London W1

On the first floor of the Trocadero there is a beautiful frieze of King Arthur.
www.londontrocadero.com

Westminter Abbey
London SW1

Westminster Abbey has many stunning features including a lovely mosaic of the Last Supper at the High Altar that was designed in 1867 by Sir Giles Gilbert Scot. The great Cosmati pavement at the Abbey is magnificent the complexity and subtlety of the design and workmanship can be seen nowhere else on this scale.
www.westminster-abbey.org

Design Other

* Central St Martin's
Fountains and Outdoor Art
Kings Cross N1
Situated at Granary Square the stunning
fountain has over 1000 individually
programmed water jets.
www.csm.arts.ac.uk

Cleopatra's Needle
Victoria Embankment WC2
A genuine Ancient Egyptian obelisks, however
somewhat misnamed as it has no particular
connection with Queen Cleopatra Queen of
Egypt. The London "needle" was originally
made during the reign of the 18th Dynasty
Pharaoh Thutmose III but was falsely named
"Cleopatra's needle".

Dorchester Hotel Park Lane W1
Designed in the 1930's by Sir Owen Williams,
some of the key glories of The Dorchester were
only added in the 1950s by the theatrical
designer Oliver Messel. The Promenade with
its cosy seating and stunning palm trees was
refurbished in 2005 by Thierry Despont.
www.thedorchester.com

Interesting Fact
The Dorchester
The London Plane tree in the front garden of
the Dorchester was named one of the 'Great
Trees of London' by The London Tree Forum.

Eltham Palace London SE9

Immerse yourself in 1930s Art Deco decadence at Eltham Palace, one of the most enchanting visitor attractions in London. It's among the finest examples of Art Deco architecture in England.

Thrifty Tip
Eltham Palace

The Garden and Outside of Eltham Palace can be visited for only £6.
www.english-heritage.org.uk

Fortnum and Mason Clock London W1

The ornate clock over the front entrance to F&M has eighteen bells that chime every 15 minutes. On the hour, doors open and four foot high figures of Mr. Fortnum and Mr. Mason appear. They bow to each other, check standards, turn around and go back inside.
www.fortnumandmason.com

Interesting Fact
Fortnum and Mason

Charles Drury Edward Fortnum (1820–1899) of the family, was a distinguished art collector and a Trustee of the British Museum, to which he donated his collection of Islamic ceramics.

Horses of Helios Haymarket W1

The Four bronze Horses of Helios stood in a beautiful fountain, were created in 1992 by sculptor Rudy Weller they are based on the Greek God of the sun (Helios).

K2 Red Telephone Box London
The iconic K2 Red Telephone Boxes were designed by Sir Giles Gilbert Scott. Although no longer in use you can still find two K2 phone boxes at the entrance to the Royal Academy of Arts.

National Gallery Trafalgar Square WC2
Set into the floor of the first landing in the National Gallery's Portico entrance is 'The Awakening of the Muses', a marble mosaic laid in 1933 by the Russian-born artist Boris Anrep.
www.nationalgallery.org.uk

Interesting Fact
National Gallery
Artstart
ArtStart is the National Gallery's award-winning interactive multimedia system, where you can explore the collection for information on every painting in the Gallery via easy to use touch-screens.

Paddington Station London W2
Paddington Station was designed by Brunel, who was later commemorated by a statue on the station concourse. The station opened in 1854. The spectacular glazed roof is supported by wrought iron arches and the roof is 210m long.

Red Letter Box (Pillar Box)
Royal Mail London
The advent of the British letter box can be traced to Sir Rowland Hill Secretary of the Post Office and his Surveyor.

Interesting Fact Letter Box
Sir Rowland Hill's surveyor happened to be
noted novelist Anthony Trollope.

* Interesting Fact
GOLD Letter Boxes
Royal Mail has painted more than 100 of its
iconic red post boxes gold to celebrate every
Team GB and Paralympics GB gold medal won
during London 2012 Olympic Games and
Paralympic Games. The boxes have been
placed in the Towns where the athletes are
from.

Reformers Tree Mosaic Hyde Park W2
The Reformers Tree Mosaic in Hyde Park
commemorates a tree that was burnt down
during reform riots in 1866.

Serpentine Gallery
Pavilion Commision
London W2
The annual Pavilion commission is a program
of temporary structures by internationally
acclaimed architects and designers and is one of
the most anticipated events on the cultural
calendar.

Interesting Fact
Pavilion Commision
The Serpentine Gallery Pavilion 2013 was
designed by multi award-winning Japanese
architect Sou Fujimoto.

Shad Thames
A narrow partly cobbled street linked with
latticed elevated walkways.

Sotheby's Auction House London W1
The Egyptian sculpture above the door of
Sotheby's in Mayfair is the oldest man made
object in London dating back to 1600BC.
www.sothebys.com/en.html

Interesting Fact
Southerby's
In 2004 Southerby's set the record for any work
of art at auction when Pablo Piccasso's *Garson*
with a Pipe sold in New York for $104.2
Million.

Traffic Light Tree
The Traffic Light Tree is 8 meters tall and
contains 75 sets of traffic lights.
www.towerhamlets.gov.uk

Please Note
The Traffic Light Tree is looking for a new site
having been removed from its previous position
on Heron Quay roundabout as part of a major
improvement scheme for the junction. To find
out the tree's new position visit the website
www.towerhamlets.gov.uk

Interesting Fact
Traffic Light Tree
Isle of Dogs

The Traffic Light tree was created by French sculptor Pierre Vivant.

Interesting Fact
Isle of Dogs
The Isle of Dogs is so called because Tudor Monarchs kept their hunting dogs there.

Architecture Design/ Religious Buildings

Abbeys & Cathedrals

Westminster Abbey London W1
Westminster Abbey is an architectural masterpiece of the 13th to 16th centuries, and a stunningly beautiful gothic building. The Abbey contains countless memorials and effigies to the famous and great of the nation it is a must-see living pageant of British history. For centuries the Coronation of British monarchs has taken place at the Abbey.
www.Westminster-abbey.org/home

Interesting Facts
Westminster Abbey Bells
Service ringing takes place at service conclusion except when the Monarch attends when the bells are also rung beforehand. The tenor bell is tolled following the announcement of the death of a member of the Royal family and on the death of the Dean of Westminster.

Westminster Abbey Choir
The Choir is renowned worldwide as one of the
finest choirs of its type, comprising of 30 boys
(all of whom attend the Abbey's dedicated
Choir School) and 12 professional adult singers.
The Choir plays a central role both in the daily
choral services in the Abbey and in the many
royal, state and national occasions which take
place there.

Coronation Chair
The coronation chair at the Abbey was made on
the orders of King Edward I and dates back to
1300–1. The Coronation chair has undergone
conservation and can now be seen in St
George's chapel, at the west end of the nave.

Famous Burials
Westminster Abbey
Some of the most famous to lie at the Abbey
include the poets John Dryden, Tennyson,
Robert Browning and John Masefield. Many
writers, including William Camden, Dr Samuel
Johnson, Charles Dickens Richard Brinsley
Sheridan, Rudyard Kipling and Thomas Hardy
are also buried here.

Royal Weddings
Highlights of recent years have included the
Wedding of Their Royal Highnesses the Duke
and Duchess of Cambridge (William & Kate) in
April 2011.

Thrifty Tip
Westminster Abbey
Visit the Abbey during Evensong where you can hear the beautiful Westminster Choir - the Queens Choristers. Evensong is held on Monday, Tuesday, Thursday, and Friday at 5pm and Sunday at 3pm see website:
FREE to visit the Abbey during
www.Westminster-abbey.org/home

St Paul's Cathedral London EC4
St Paul's with its world-famous dome is an iconic feature of the London skyline. The present church dates from the late 17th century and was built to an English Baroque design by Sir Christopher Wren, assisted by Nicholas Hawksmoor.
FREE to visit St Paul's during Evensong
www.stpauls.co.uk

Interesting Facts
St Paul's Cathedral

The Whispering Gallery
The whispering gallery constructed around the dome allows whispers from one part of the gallery to be audible to a listener with an ear held to the wall at any other point around the gallery.

Woodcarvings and Mosaics
Sir James Thornhill painted the eight paintings of the life of St Paul that line the interior of the dome. The man responsible for the woodwork, including the choir stalls is the amazing woodcarver Grinling Gibbons.

Royal Wedding
Prince Charles and Lady Diana Spencer were married at St Paul's Cathedral on 29 July 1981.

Thrifty Tip
St Paul's Cathedral
Visit St Paul's during Evensong where you can hear the beautiful St Paul's Choir. Held on Monday, Tuesday, Wednesday, Thursday, and Friday at 5pm and Sunday at 3.15pm. See website:

The full ring of bells is normally rung each Sunday see website for timings.

Southwark Cathedral London SE1
There has been a church on the site since AD 606. Southwark Cathedral is the oldest cathedral church building in London, and archaeological evidence shows there was Roman pagan worship there.

Interesting Fact
Harvard Memorial Chapel
Southwark Cathedral
The Harvard Memorial Chapel at Southwark Cathedral was named after Southwarks most famous emigrant John Harvard, the founder of Harvard University USA.
www.cathedral.southwark.anglican.org

Thrifty Tip
Southwark Cathedral
The Cathedral Choir was formed in 1848.

The Choir plays a special part in the Cathedral's community involvement and sings at the weekly Choral Mass see website for details:
www.southwark-rc-cathedral.org.uk

Churches

Brompton Oratory Kensington SW3
Italian Renaissance style Roman Catholic Church where Roman Baroque and Wren are also drawn on. The Church has beautiful carvings in metalwork, plasterwork, wood and stone, and it houses notable Italian Baroque sculpture
www.bromptonoratory.com

Interesting Fact
Brompton Oratory:
Legend has it that KGB spy's used the church to leave messages for each other.

Thrifty Tip
Brompton Oratory FREE Organ Recitals
The Oratory is a unique musical establishment comprising three separate choirs and professional music staff.
FREE Organ Recitals are also performed see website for full details.
www.bromptonoratory.com

Chiswick Russian Orthodox Church London W4
This church opened its doors in 1998. It is a square, white building with very impressive woodwork on the outside.

The distinctive onion shaped dome is painted blue with gold stars. Inside there is an ornate screen running the width of the Church in front of the altar.
www.russianchurchlondon.org/en

St Bartholemew the Great
Saint Bartholomew the Great is one of London's oldest churches. It was founded in 1123 as an Augustinian Priory and has been in use as a place of worship since at least 1143. It is an active Anglican/Episcopal Church.
www.greatstbarts.com

Interesting Fact
St Bartholemew the Great Lady Chapel
The Lady Chapel at the east end was previously used for commercial purposes and it was there that Benjamin Franklin served a year as journeyman printer.

St Brides Church Fleet Street London EC4
The Church was designed in 1672 by Sir Christopher Wren. St Brides Church is in Fleet Street (the home of the British press). Because of its location the Church has a long association with journalists and newspapers.
www.stbrides.com

Interesting Facts
St Brides Church
St Brides is well known for its distinctive spire. The spire is said to have provided inspiration for the traditional tiered wedding cake.

The famous Diariest Samuel Pepys was baptised at St Brides.

St James Piccadilly London W1
An Anglican parish church built in 1684 and designed by Sir Christoper Wren, the church is one of Wren's most famous churches.

Interesting Fact
St James
The famous poet William Blake was baptised there.

Thrifty Tip
St James FREE lunchtime recitals
Monday, Wednesday & Fridays see website for listings.
www.st-james-piccadilly.org

St Lawrence Jewry London EC2
St Lawrence was first built in 1136 it was destroyed in the Great Fire of London in 1666, and rebuilt in 1677 by Wren. The Church was badly damaged in the Second World War but faithfully reconstructed afterwards.

Interesting Fact
St Lawrence Jewry
The Church is the official church of the Lord Mayor of London.

Thrifty Tip
St Lawrence Jewry
FREE Piano Concerts
See website for listings.
www.stlawrencejewry.org.uk

St Margarets Westminster London SW1
Standing between Westminster Abbey and the
Houses of Parliament, and commonly called
the parish church of the House of Commons,
St Margaret's has witnessed many important
events.
www.Westminster-abbey.org/st-margarets

Interesting Facts
St Margaret's
Diarist Samuel Pepys & former Prime Minister
Sir Winston Churchill both married at St
Margarets.

Field of Remembrance
St Margarets
Since 1928 the churchyard has been the setting
every November for the Field of Remembrance
organised by the Royal British Legion Poppy
Factory. The churchyard is divided into plots
which are assigned to the military and civilian
services. Relatives and old comrades are able to
remember those who died in war by planting a
poppy cross in the appropriate plot.
www.Westminster-abbey.org/st-margarets

Thrifty Tip
St Margarets
FREE Recitals &
FREE Carol Services
FREE Recitals during the summer, and they
also have FREE Carol Services in December
for full listings see the website:
www.Westminster-abbey.org/st-margarets

St Martins in the fields
Trafalgar Square London WC2
St Martin-in-the-Fields is a busy working church
with over 20 services and 6-7concerts per week.
St Martin's has a commitment to discovering,
nurturing and promoting new and emerging
talent manifest through the Lunchtime
Concerts.
www.smitf.org

Thrifty Tip
St Martins in the fields
FREE Lunchtime Concerts
See website for full listings:
www.smitf.org

St Mary Abbots Church
Kensington London W8
George Gilbert Scott RA (later Sir George) was
the architect, for St Mary Abbots Church. On
entering the church, one's first impression is
probably of its cathedral-like size. The reredos
is of alabaster, marble and Italian mosaics with
pictorial panels of the four Evangelists.
www.smanews.weebly.com

Healing St Mary Abbots Church
Eucharist's of Healing with laying-on of hands
and anointing are held on the Third Thursday
of each month at 2pm.

Interesting Fact
St Mary Abbots Church
Until the early 19th century Mary Abbots was
the only church in Kensington.

St Mary Abbots had many eminent parishioners including Sir Isaac Newton, William Wilberforce (the famous anti slave campaigner), William Thackeray and Beatrix Potter.

Thrifty Tip
St Mary Abbots Church
Visit the St Mary Abbots tower (designed by Sir Giles Gilbert Scott) and see the bells being rung. Visitors are welcome on Sunday mornings when they ring from 8.45 to 9.30 and on Thursday evenings during practice from 7.30 to 9.15. The tower is on the North side of the Church see website.

St Marylebone Church London NW1
Thomas Hardwick Jnr (1752-1827) became a notable church architect and the church of St Mary's is his finest piece of work. The building is a prime example of Regency architecture. This was the fourth church building on the site.
www.stmarylebone.org

Interesting Facts
St Marylebone
Thomas Hardwick Jnr
In his later years Hardwick became a tutor to none other than JMW Tuner whom he persuaded to concentrate more on painting rather than architecture.

Nelson & Dickens were parishioners and Lord Byron were baptised at St Marylebone.

Robert Browning and Elizabeth Barrett Married at the church in 1846 (Their marriage certificate is preserved in the church archives). There is a Commemorative window dedicated to Browning and Barrett and busts of the pair.
www.stmarylebone.org

Interesting Fact
Elizabeth Barrett Browning
The sonnet, *"How Do I Love Thee,"* was written by Elizabeth Barrett Browning for Robert Browning.

Healing Prayer at Marylebone Church
There are services of Prayer for Healing offered at this church see website for full details.
 Also an informal healing prayer group meets at 2.30 - 4 pm on the 1st Friday afternoon each month.

Thrifty Tip
St Marylebone Church
FREE Organ Recitals
Students from the Royal Academy of Music regularly play this Rieger Organ and organ recitals are given by the Church organists. These are advertised outside the Church

St Mary Le Bow London EC2
Founded in or around 1080 as the London headquarters of the archbishops of Canterbury, this medieval church survived three devastating collapses before being completely destroyed in the Great Fire of 1666.

Rebuilt by Sir Christopher Wren, it was destroyed once more in 1941 but was again rebuilt and re-consecrated in 1964.
www.stmarylebow.co.uk

Interesting Fact
St Mary Le Bow
According to tradition a true "Cockney" (Londoner) must be born within the sound of Bow Bells.

Thrifty Tip
St Mary Le Bow
FREE Recitals
FREE Live Chamber Music & FREE organ recitals see website for listings.
www.stmarylebow.co.uk

St Paul's Covent Garden London WC2
The Actors Church
The Parish Church of Covent Garden is also affectionately known as the Actors church because of its long association with the theatre community. This beautiful church was built by Inigo Jones and has been there since 1633.
www.actorschurch.org

Interesting Facts
St Paul's Covent Garden
Many famous names have been connected with St Paul's John Wesley preached here, J.M.W Turner and W.S Gilbert were baptised here, and those buried here include Sir Peter Lely, Samuel Butler, William Wycherly, Grinling Gibbons, Thomas Arne, and Thomas Rowlandson.

St Paul's Churchyard

The first known victim of the 1665–1666 outbreak of the plaque in England, Margaret Ponteous was buried in the churchyard on 12 April 1665.

Temple Church London EC4

The Church was built by the Knights Templar, in the 12th century. This is the church of the Inner and Middle Temple, two of England's four ancient societies of lawyers. They also welcome visitors from all over the world to this beautiful and historic place at the very centre of London.

Thrifty Tip
Temple Church

Admission FREE under 18s, senior citizens and to those who would like to say a prayer and during evensong
www.templechurch.com

Wesley's Chapel London EC1

Has a thriving Methodist congregation in the heart of London with a full programme of services and events throughout the week.
www.wesleyschapel.org.uk

Thrifty Tip Wesley's Chapel
FREE lunchtime recitals on Tuesdays

Convent

Tyburn Convent London W1

Tyburn Convent is a monastery situated right in the heart of London. It is a cloistered community of Benedictine contemplatives who live by the ancient monastic Rule of St. Benedict.

www.tyburnconvent.org.uk

Thrifty Tips
Tyburn Convent

The Nuns choir sings mass at the Convent seven times per day, their voices are beautiful and this is a magical experience, for up to date times see website.

Tyburn Convent
FREE Talks

There are FREE talks about the Convent at The Crypt daily see website for details:

www.tyburnconvent.org.uk

Floating Church

St Peters Barge
(Floating Church)

St Peter's Barge is London's only floating church, located in the heart of Canary Wharf. Their aim is to help all people know God better.

www.stpetersbarge.org

Temples

Buddhapadipa Temple London SW19

This Thai Buddhist Temple is home to monks and nuns. The Temple welcomes visitors of any faith to view the grounds and temple as long as they are respectful.
www.buddhapadipa.org

London Buddhist Centre London E2

The London Buddhism Centre offers visitors the opportunity to learn to meditate. The project offers mindfulness-based approaches to well-being.

Thrifty Tip
London Buddhist Centre FREE taster session in Breathing Space

See website for full details
www.lbc.org.uk/daymeditation.asp

Neasden Temple London NW10

BAPS Shri Swaminarayan Mandir popularly known as the Neasden Temple is the first traditional Hindu Mandir in Europe. The Temple is a masterpiece of exotic design.

This stunning architectural masterpieces was created from the conceptual design and vision of His Holiness Pramukh Swami Maharaji, and the architect C. B. Sompura and his team.
www.mandir.org

**Shri Vallabh Nidhi Hindu Temple
Wembley**
The architecture of SVN presents an epitome of mystical scales and proportions along with the heavenly carving which turns the structure into a magnificent celestial body. The temple plays the role of a place of deep relaxation and is visited by thousands each year.
www.svnuk.org/our-temples/wembley-temple

Other Religious Buildings

**Bevis Marks Synagogue
London EC3**
The Oldest Synagogue in Britain built in 1701. The synagogue's most prominent feature is the beautiful Renaissance style ark located at the centre of the Eastern wall of the building.

**Interesting Fact
Bevis Marks Synagogue**
The birth of Benjamin Disraeli (Britain's first Jewish born Prime Minister) is recorded in the synagogues registry.
www.bevismarks.org.uk

**Battersea Park Peace Pagoda
London SW11**
One of the major landmarks in Battersea Park is the beautiful Peace Pagoda.
www.batterseapark.org

Interesting Fact
Battersea Park Peace Pagoda
A team of 50 volunteers and Buddhist monks and nuns of the Nipponzan Myohoji Buddhist Order constructed the Peace Pagoda which is used as a place of worship by many.
www.batterseapark.org

London Central Mosque
Regents Park London NW8
Designed by Sir Frederick Gibberd and completed in 1978, it has a prominent golden dome. The main hall can hold over five thousand worshippers. The inside of the dome is decorated with broken shapes in the Islamic tradition.
www.iccuk.org

* Interesting Fact
Sir Frederick Gibberd
Sir Frederick Gibberd also designed Harlow New Town in Essex, his home and his private garden can be visited.
Admission Concessions £3 Adults £4
www.thegibberdgarden.co.uk

Methodist Central Hall Westminster
London SW1
The Church at Methodist Central Hall Westminster is a culturally diverse fellowship their mission is to be a vital Christian presence in the heart of London.
www.methodist-central-hall.org.uk

Interesting Fact
Methodist Central Hall
William Lloyd Webber (father of Andrew &
Julian) was the Director of music at Central hall
and he also played the stunning Great Hall
Organ there.

Methodist Central Hall
Healing
There are regular services of Prayer for Healing
of Body, Mind & Spirit with the laying-on of
hands see website for details:
www.methodist-central-hall.org.uk

Section 3
Farms, Parks and Woods

Section 3

Farms Gardens Parks & Woods

Farms

London City Farms Admission FREE

London's City Farms provide communities and visitors with the opportunity to connect with animals and nature and enjoy a taste of country life in the city. The city farms have sheep, goats, cows, alpacas, pigs and various poultry. There are many animals to see some of which you can feed or stroke at certain times of the week. See individual farm websites below for full details:

* Alexander Palace Deer Enclosure
London N22

Alexandra Mackenzie included a small deer enclosure when he designed the original layout of the park. Fallow deer were reintroduced to Alexandra Park and the small herd today are their direct descendents.
www.alexandrapalace.com

* Deen City Farm
London Wimbledon SW19

Deen City Farm is a unique, educational resource and registered charity. The farm gives people the opportunity to learn from their visit, and to contribute to a community project.
Admission FREE
www.deencityfarm.co.uk

Interesting Fact
Deen City Farm
The Fizzy Bottle Roof Project at Deen City
Farm turned 7000 plastic bottles into a roof.
The bottle roof was designed and orchestrated
by William Waterhouse and Louisa Loakes.

* Freightliners City Farm London N7
Freightliners Farm in the heart of Islington
provides an exciting opportunity for visitors to
experience a real working farm in action.
Admission FREE
www.freightlinersfarm.org.uk

* Hackney City Farm London E2
Hackney City Farm offers children and adults
the opportunity to get up close to a range of
farmyard animals.
Admission FREE
www.hackneycityfarm.co.uk

* Kentish Town City Farm London NW3
Pony Rides are one of the highlights of Kentish
Town City Farm. The rides are
for children over the age of four, they take place
on Saturday & Sunday at 1:30pm £2 per ride.
Admission FREE
www.ktcityfarm.org.uk

Thrifty Tip
Kentish Town City Farm
Art sessions, baking, creating & rhyme-time
parents with 0-5yrs, and Pottery sessions all ages
welcome small Fee.

See website for full details:
www.ktcityfarm.org.uk

* Mudchute London City Farm
Mudchute is the largest inner City Farm
anywhere in Europe (32 acres). The farm has a
collection of British rare breeds and over 200
animals and fowl.
www.mudchute.org

* Newham City Farm London E6
Visit Blaze the Shire horse, taste the honey
made in our beehives, and buy some fresh farm
eggs when you come down to the farm.
Admission FREE
**www.community-links.org/local-
services/city-farm**

* Spitalfields City Farm London E1
The Farmyard is home to many much loved
animals including great characters such as
Bayleaf the Donkey & Bramble the Goat.
Admission FREE
www.spitalfieldscityfarm.org

* Surrey Docks Farm London SE16
Surrey Docks Farm is a working city farm.
Animals reared on the farm include a herd of
milking goats, sheep, cattle, pigs, ducks, geese,
chickens, turkeys, and donkeys.
Admission FREE
www.surreydocksfarm.org.uk

*** Victoria Park Deer Enclosure
London E3**
The city's first public park, it was opened in the
East End in 1845. The park is known as the
Regents Park of the East End. The deer
enclosure is very popular with and children and
adults alike.
**Admission FREE
www.towerhamlets.gov.uk**

* Vauxhall City Farm London SE11
The farm has a therapy riding centre, education
and youth projects, a horticultural therapy
group and an award winning collection
of animals including a number of rare breeds.
**Admission FREE
www.vauxhallcityfarm.org**

*** Thrifty Tip
The Spinners
Vauxhall City Farm London SE11**
See the Spinners at Vauxhall City Farm, a group
of textile artists and craftsmen with an interest
in natural dyes and fibres.
Every Saturday 10-2pm

*** Thrifty Tip
City Farms
FREE Workshops**
Many of them have FREE workshops and
activities during school holidays.

Gardens

Barge & Dock Gardens

** Downings Road Barge Gardens
London SE1

The floating barge gardens at Downings Road Moorings were devised by the architect and moorings owner, Nick Lacey. The gardens have community value as the beautiful living walkways that tie the moorings together. They are interesting as living and floating roofs, which shows that it is possible to grow a mature garden in relatively little soil.

* Island Gardens London E14

Island Gardens is a public park located at the southern end of the Isle of Dogs on the north bank of the River Thames.

Interesting Fact
Island Gardens

It is notable for its spectacular cross-river view of the classical buildings of the former Greenwich Hospital the National Maritime Museum and the beautiful Greenwich Park.. The modern day view from Island Gardens is that of Caneletto's painting "A view of Greenwich from the River".

Botanical Healing & Peace Gardens

Battersea Park Peace Pagoda
London SW11

One of the major landmarks in Battersea Park is the Peace Pagoda. A team of 50 volunteers and Buddhist monks and nuns of the Nipponzan Myohoji Buddhist Order constructed the Peace Pagoda which is used as a place of worship by many.
www.batterseapark.org

Charlton House Charlton
London SE7

One of the CH gardens was opened in July 2006 as a Peace Garden, in conjunction with Amnesty International. The Peace Garden is open daily from 10am to 5pm in the summer or until dusk in the winter.
Admission FREE
www.royalgreenwich.gov.uk

Chelsea Physic Garden
London SW3

Chelsea Physic Garden has a unique living collection of around 5,000 different edible, useful, medicinal and historical plants. This 'hidden gem' is also a peaceful green oasis in which to enjoy a relaxing stroll.
Admission £6.00 Concessions and Children (5-15 years old)
www.chelseaphysicgarden.co.uk

**Cloisters Garden Westminster Abbey
London SW1**
Cloisters garden was used by the monks for meditation and exercise.
www.Westminster-abbey.org/visit-us/abbey-gardens

**Fulham Palace Museum
London SW6**
The beautiful Tudor Fulham Palace's ancient, botanical gardens extend 70 acres, and are open daily from dawn until dusk.
**Admission FREE
www.fulhampalace.org**

*** Horniman Museum Garden
Forest Hill London SE23**
Explore the links between plants and medicine, food, materials and dyes, watch performances on the bandstand, play music in the sound garden, relax in glorious surroundings and see stunning views over London in the award-winning 16 acre gardens, with beautiful sundials.
**Admission FREE
www.horniman.ac.uk**

*** Thrifty Tip
Horniman Museum**
During AUG/SEPT their popular storytellers bring their collections and gardens alive with enchanting stories from around the world.
www.horniman.ac.uk

**Royal College of Physicians
Medical Garden London NW1**

The RCP has had a medicinal garden since 1965. From March to November, the RCP offers tours of the medicinal garden on the first Wednesday of every month at 2pm.
Admission FREE
www.rcplondon.ac.uk/museum-and-garden

St Ethelbergs Centre for Reconcilliation & Peace London EC2
This used to be a church; the derelict land behind the old church is now a peace garden with small fountain and beautiful mosaic tiling. This quiet little garden was designed by Sylvia Crawford and has a Moroccan feel the Centerpiece is the peace tent (yurt).
www.stethelburgas.org

Interesting Fact
St Ethelbergs
A special breed of rose grows in the garden St Ethelbergs which was specifically cultivated for the church.

Thrifty Tip
FREE Events St Ethelbergs
The centre runs many FREE Events including Healing see website for full details:
www.stethelburgas.org

Tavistock Square Herb Garden London WC1
Tavistock Square Gardens include fine mature trees and shrubs around the border and lawns and flower beds in the centre.

There are also plants suitable for medicinal use mainly herbs.
www.camden.gov.uk

Tibetan Peace Garden at Imperial War Museum London SE1

As part of creating a greater awareness of Tibetan culture and promoting HH the Dalai Lama's message of peace. It has a very elaborate artistic design of a Kalachakra Mandala as the centrepiece in a modern setting of western sculpture. It has now become a popular Tibetan landmark in the heart of London.
www.iwm.org.uk

Interesting Fact Tibetan Peace Garden

The Peace Garden was commissioned by Tibet Foundation and built on land provided by Southwark Council. It has been donated to the people of Britain for all to enjoy.
www.tibetfoundation.org

Kitchen Gardens

* Calthorpe Community London WC1

An inner city oasis, a community garden and centre where people grow and learn together taking care of each other and the environment. Families with young children meet and learn together through play.
www.calthorpeproject.org.uk

* Thrifty Tip
Calthorpe Community
FREE Activities
Holiday, after-school and weekend programmes
provide outdoor, creative and social activities
for children, including Art, Cooking, Growing,
Tree Climbing and more see website for full
details:
Admission FREE
www.calthorpeproject.org.uk

* Clissold Park
Kitchen Garden London N16
Organic market gardens run by Growing
Communities. The site is open to the public
every Tuesday (Feb-Dec) when the grower is
working there.
www.clissoldpark.com

* Culpeper Community Garden
London N1
Culpeper Community Garden is a beautiful
public open space in the heart of Islington
which serves both as a city park and as an
environmental community project. Managed by
and for local people, it is a unique project where
people come together to appreciate and
enhance their environment.
www.culpeper.org.uk

* Global Generation Garden
Honey Project Kings X London N1
The Honey Club is a social enterprise set up by
Wolff Olins and Global Generation.

They have two beehives on the roof of the Wolff Olins building, and now have 100,000 honeybees living by their roof garden.
www.globalgeneration.org.uk

* Grow Heathrow London

Transition Heathrow is an abandoned market garden site in Sipson; one of the villages to be completely resurfaced to make way for a third runway at Heathrow. The site has been transformed into a beacon of community strength and a great example of how to live sustainably on this planet.
www.transitionheathrow.com

* Thrifty Tip
Grow Heathrow
FREE Crafternoons and
FREE Gardening Club

This wonderful project offers various FREE regular events including crafternoon's and gardening club.
There is also a Bicycle workshop where the only charge is a small donation see website:
www.transitionheathrow.com/grow-heathrow

* Hackney City Farm Garden London E2

Hackney City Farm offers children and adults the opportunity to get up close to a range of farmyard animals. See, smell and plant vegetables and other food plants; and learn new skills to live a healthier, happier life with a lower environmental impact.
www.hackneycityfarm.co.uk

* Kings Cross Skip Garden

The King's Cross Central Skip Garden is a self-sustaining vegetable garden with a twist - its moveable. As different areas in King's Cross Central are developed the skips will be moved. The Skip Garden has been created and gardened by volunteers from the Guardian and the Observer, young people from the area and construction apprentices.

www.kingscrosscentral.com/skip_garden

*** Spitalfields City Farm
Kitchen Garden London E1
FREE Pick and Cook Sessions** are an opportunity to learn how to cook using garden produce to create tasty, interesting and nutritious meals, and to share food in a friendly setting.

www.spitalfieldscityfarm.org

* The Regent's Park Allotment Garden

Open to the public Monday to Friday. They run special open days with activities, competitions, games and the opportunity to ask questions about the garden, food-growing, and Capital Growth.

www.royalparks.org.uk/parks

*** Waterlow Park Kitchen Garden
London N6**

The Kitchen Garden was opened for the enjoyment of the public with plots being run by a number of community groups.

www.waterlowpark.org.uk

Westminster Abbey College Garden
London SW1

The College Garden was the Infirmary's Garden, used for the purposes of growing medicinal herbs and foods for the general well-being of the occupants of the Abbey. It is very unusual (possibly unique in England) for an Abbey or Monastery to still have its infirmary's garden attached and kept as a garden.

Interesting Fact
College Garden
Westminster Abbey London SW1

London's Oldest Garden originally was part of the infirmary garden used for growing medicinal plants, herbs and vegetables.

www.westminster-abbey.org

Thrifty Tip
College Garden
Westminster Abbey

Lunchtime concerts are held in the gardens during the summer months.

Private Gardens

The National Garden Scheme
Open Gardens

Every year NGS gardens across England and Wales welcome about 750,000 visitors. Most gardens which open for the NGS are privately owned. Some gardens open as part of a group with the whole community involved.

Visiting the Gardens costs on average £3 and all money raised goes to charity, for further details visit the website:
www.ngs.org.uk

Roof Gardens

Brunel Museum Midnight Apothecary
FREE Events
The Midnight Apothecary brings it's pop up cocktail bar to the Museum's rooftop garden. A roof gardens above the Thames Tunnel.
Admission FREE
www.brunel-museum.org.uk

Kensington Roof Gardens London W8
The beautiful Garden is owned by Virgin and is open to the public unless there is a private event.

It has many species of plants, a stream with ducks flamingos and more.
Telephone before making a visit
0207 737 7994
www.roofgardens.virgin.com

* One New Change
Roof Garden London EC4
There is a sunken garden, an oasis of leafy calm on the busy corner of Cheapside and New Change along with Green roof areas - a series of stepped terraces - that will encourage biodiversity in the centre of London.
www.onenewchange.com

* Queen Elizabeth Hall Roof Garden
Southbank SE1
The Queen Elizabeth Hall Roof Garden was designed by the Eden Project. You can relax in this beautiful garden which has amazing views of London. The Queen Elizabeth Hall Roof Gardens opens daily until dusk.
Admission FREE
www.southbankcentre.co.uk

* Thrifty Tip
Southbank Centre
Queen Elizabeth Hall Fountains
Jeppe Hein's "Appearing Rooms" fountain is outside Queen Elizabeth Hall Southbank Centre. The fountain is great fun for children of all ages, and a fantastic fun way to cool off on a hot summer's day.

School of Oriental and African Studies
Roof Garden London WC1
The Japanese-inspired roof garden at SOAS, University of London was built during the Japan 2001 celebrations. It provides an area away from the noise and bustle of London streets, where visitors can relax and meditate.
www.soas.ac.uk

Garden Squares

* Open Garden Squares Weekend
A magical two-day event where community gardens and private squares throughout London welcome visitors from around the world.

See website for full details:
www.opensquares.org

Tavistock Square
London WC2
A number of memorial features can be found in
Tavistock Square, including some which
promote peace. There is the central statue of
Mahatma Gandhi that brings visitors and
pilgrims from around the world. There is also a
garden dedicated to the Bloomsbury Set
Novalist Virginia Woolf.

Interesting Fact
Mahatma Gandhi
At the age of 18 in 1888, Gandhi went to
nearby University College London to study law
and train as a barrister.

Wildlife Gardens

* Barbican Centre
London Silk Street EC2
The Barbican Centre has the second biggest
Conservatory in London; explore the hidden
tropical oasis in the heart of the city. It is home
to finches, quails, and exotic fish and over 2,000
species of tropical plants and trees.
www.barbican.org.uk

* Barnsbury Wood London N1
Barnsbury Wood was originally a garden
belonging to George Thornhill who built the
surrounding houses in the 1840s.

The area was eventually abandoned to nature and then became a woodland, wildlife garden and London's smallest Nature Reserve.
www.islington.gov.uk

* Natural History Museum
Wildlife Garden London SW7

The NHS Wildlife Garden is home to 1000s of British plant and animal species throughout the seasons. Dragonflies, moorhens, moths, butterflies, foxes, robins, marsh marigolds, primroses, lime, hornbeam, and even sheep are just some of the abundant species that live in and visit the garden.
Admission FREE
www.nhm.ac.uk

Gardens Other

* London Fields
London E8

Has Ping Pong Tables, Boules pits, and a refurbished Lido (a great place to swim).

Royal Hospital Chelsea Garden
London SW3

Royal Hospital Chelsea is home to "The Men in Scarlet', the Chelsea Pensioners. Visit the stunning 66 acre garden a beautiful green retreat.
Admission FREE
www.chelsea-pensioners.co.uk/home

Southside House London SW19

Wilderness, order, woodland, secret pathways, classical follies and water all combine to create a garden of surprises at Southside House. Wildlife is encouraged at Southside. The gardens are a series of sculptural rooms linked by water and mysterious pathways.
Admission Children £2.50 Students Concessions £4 Adults £5
www.southsidehouse.com/pages/aboutsou thsideho.html

Interesting Fact
Southside House

The house has connections with Queen Anne Boleyn, the Duke of Wharton, Frederick, Prince of Wales, Marie Antoinette, Admiral Lord Nelson, Lady Hamilton and others. See website for full details:
www.southsidehouse.com/pages/aboutsou thsideho.html

St Dunstains in the East London EC3

This garden is spectacular with its ornamental vines, exotic plants, cobbled paths and bright flowers. The gardens are set in the ruins of a Wren church. This is a beautiful green space.

Interesting Fact
St Dunstains in the East
Insect Hotel

Look out for the winning Insect Hotel built within the garden as part of the 2010 Beyond the Hive competition.

Tavistock Square Gardens

The Gardens include fine mature trees and shrubs around the border and lawns and flower beds in the centre. A number of memorial features can be found including some which promote peace.

There is the central statue of Mahatma Gandhi, a tree planted to commemorate the victims of the Hiroshima bombing and a Conscientious Objectors' memorial stone.

The Fan Museum Secret Japanese Garden
London SE10

The Orangery overlooks a "secret" garden in the Japanese manner, with a fan shaped parterre, pond, stream and oriental architectural features.

Children £3 Adults £4

Admission FREE for OAPs and Disabled on Tuesday afternoon see website.
www.thefanmuseum.org.uk

Thrifty Tip
Fan Museum

Afternoon teas are served on Tuesdays and Sundays from 3pm.

Prices for Tea £5.00 (half tea) or £6.00 (full tea)
www.thefanmuseum.org.uk

The Rookery Stretham Common
London SW16

The modern Rookery contains an ornamental pond, flower and herbaceous beds and a rock garden with streams.

With areas of woodland important for biodiversity and environmental education, the place bristles with birdsong and wildlife, and is a delightful place to spend some reflective moments.

Thrifty Tip
The Rookery
In the summer the lawns of the Rookery are used as an open air theatre where Shakespeare plays are performed.
www.lambeth.gov.uk

Victoria Embankment Gardens London
Victoria Embankment gardens are part of the Thames Embankment. The river side of the gardens is lined with mature trees, and grass and flower beds are spread throughout the gardens.
www.westminster.gov.uk

Thrifty Tip
Victoria Embankment Gardens
FREE Concerts & Deckchairs
Victoria Embankment Gardens is a lovely spot by the Thames to have a picnic lunch on the deckchairs or grass.

Thrifty Tip
Victoria Embankment Gardens
There are also number of summer lunch-time concerts in the Bandstand area.

Victoria Tower Garden
London SW1
Victoria Tower Gardens lies at the heart of Westminster, bordered by the Houses of Parliament, the River Thames, Millbank and Lambeth Bridge. It is a lovely grassed area that overlooks the Thames.

Interesting Facts
Victoria Tower Garden
Fountain
Victoria Tower Garden has a fountain commemorating the end of slavery.

Victoria Tower Garden &
Emmeline Pankhurst
The garden has a statue of the political activist and British leader of the suffragette movement Emmeline Pankhurst, the movement helped British women win the vote.

Thrifty Tip
Garden Museum
London SE1
If you like gardens you will enjoy the garden Museum set up in 1977 in order to rescue from demolition the abandoned ancient church of St Mary's which is the burial place of John Tradescant, the first great gardener and plant-hunter in British history.
Admission £3 Students/Concessions £4 Senior Citizens £5 Adults
FREE for under 16s those on Jobseekers Allowance and carer's of disabled people
www.gardenmuseum.org.uk

Parks

Children's Parks

* Alexandra Park London N2

Alexandra Park is 196 acres of parkland surrounding the Palace that is open all year round. Park facilities include a Boating Lake, Deer enclosure, Ice Rink, Little Dinosaurs Ball Park, Pitch & Put, and Skate Park. www.alexandrapalace.com

Interesting Fact
Alexandra Palace
The first BBC TV Broadcast was transmitted from Alexandra Palace on 2nd November 1936..

* Aldenham Country Park
100 Aker Wood Elstree WD6

100 Aker Wood at Aldenham Country Park is where Winnie the Pooh lives with Rabbit, Eeyore and Piglet too (see website). Aldenham Country Park is a beautiful place for wildlife, rare breed animals, woodland experiences, mixed farming, pony rides, nature walks and more. It also has a rare breed's farm.

Although 12 miles from central London Aldenham Country Park is really worth a visit, it is a magical place.
www.aldenhamcountrypark.co.uk/things-to-do/100-acre-wood

* Arc in the Park London E16

Arc in the Park is a FREE inclusive adventure playground which promotes the development of children and young people (5-14 years), using out of school play activities and holiday play projects.

www.newham.gov.uk

* Battersea Park London SW11

The park has an amazing adventure playground designed for children aged 5 to 16. There is a smaller playground for younger children. The park is full of wildlife the most obvious are the birds living around the lake. Whilst feeding the ducks you will often see Herons, Cormorants and Grebes.

www.batterseaparkzoo.co.uk

* Battersea Park Childrens Zoo London SW11

Battersea Park Zoo offers an exciting animal experience. At the Zoo you can come face to face with a ring tailed lemur, or popped up right beside a meerkat. Or spend time with their Kune Kune pigs Piggle and Wiggle, or watch an otter at work. From giant rabbits to miniature Shetland ponies, monkey mayhem to the mouse house this is the zoo that gets you up close and personal.

Admission prices Children £5.50 Adults £6.95
www.batterseaparkzoo.co.uk

Interesting Facts
Battersea Park

The first Football match played under FA Rules was played in Battersea Park in 1864.

The Park Peace Pagoda

One of the major landmarks in Battersea Park is the Peace Pagoda. A team of 50 volunteers and Buddhist monks and nuns of the Nipponzan Myohoji Buddhist Order constructed the Peace Pagoda which is used as a place of worship by many.

www.batterseapark.org

* Corum's Fields London WC1

A unique seven acre playground and park for children and young people. At the back of the park there is a large adventure play area including an aerial slide. There are two large sand pits and a paddling pool in the summer.

www.coramsfields.org

* Crystal Palace Dinosaur Court London SE20

A series of sculptures of dinosaurs and extinct mammals are located in Crystal Palace Park. You can find out more about the dinosaurs at the Crystal Palace museum in the park. There is also a children's farm, a playground, a maze, an outdoor concert stage and plenty of green space to run about in.

www.crystalpalacepark.org.uk

Interesting Fact
Dinosaur Court

The sculpter of Dinosaur Court was Benjamin Waterhouse Hawkins in 1853.

Holland Park Ilchester Place W8
The Royal Borough's largest park with 22.5 hectares of gardens, children's plays facilities which include an amazing adventure playground and sports areas. There are facilities for tennis, football, golf practice nets, cricket practice nets and netball.

Thrifty Tip
Holland Park
Ecology Centre
FREE Activities
The Ecology Centre at Holland Park runs a series of events, activities and educational visits and workshops. They also run a wildlife club for children, holiday activities, and a full programmer of events for all ages.
www.rbkc.gov.uk

* Kensington Gardens London W2
Princess Diana Memorial Playground
A huge wooden pirate ship is the amazing centrepiece of this playground. This children's wonderland opened on the 30th June 2000, in memory of the late Princess Diana. This magical space has a sensory trail, tepees, a beach around the pirate ship and various toys and play sculptures; all set against a lush backdrop of trees and plants.
www.royalparks.org.uk

* Interesting Fact
Kensington Gardens
Kensington Gardens has a bronze statue of Peter Pan, the location was chosen by Peter Pan's author J.M. Barrie.

Barrie lived close to Kensington Gardens and published his first Peter Pan story in 1902 using the park as inspiration.

* Waterlow Park Highgate N6
The park has three ponds, tree lined walkways, mature shrub beds and herbaceous borders, ornamental bedding, expanses of lawn, 6 tennis courts an infant playground and a play area.
www.waterlowpark.org.uk

* Thrifty Tip
Waterlow Park
FREE Events for Families
See website for details.
www.waterlowpark.org.uk

Nature Reserves & Wildlife Gardens

Aveery Hill Winter Garden London SE9
This large open parkland with many splendid trees is notable for its winter garden (greenhouse) which is second only to Kew. The winter garden contains tropical trees and plants from around the world.

There is also a rose garden, affording a pleasant place to sit and relax.
www.royalgreenwich.gov.uk

* East Ham Nature Reserve
London E6
One of Britain's largest church yards is also a fantastic nature reserve. The church is 800 years old. The seven-acre site has been a nature reserve since 1977, providing a haven for a huge range of plants and animals.
www.community-links.org/local-services/nature-reserve

* London Wetland Centre
Barnes SW13
WWT London Wetland Centre has been voted the UK's Favourite Nature Reserve. Close to the heart of the capital, it's a haven for wildlife and people. Indulge in an afternoon of bird watching from one of the six hides. The reserve is easily accessible with pathways and bridges among the pools, meadows and gardens.
Admission Child £5.91 Concession £7.91
www.wwt.org.uk/visit/london

* Thrifty Tip
London Wetland Centre
Tours held daily at 11.30am and 2.30pm. There's no need to book and the tour.
FREE with admission

Parks Other

* Green Park London W1

Green Park is a peaceful refuge for people living working or visiting central London. It is particularly popular for sunbathing and picnics in fine weather. The paths are used extensively by joggers and runners.

www.royalparks.org.uk

* Grenwich Park London SE10

There has been a settlement on this site since Roman times. There is a large grassland enclosure covering almost 13 acres which serves as a sanctuary for deer, foxes and birds.

www.royalparks.org.uk

* Hampstead Heath
Hampstead London NW3

Hampstead Heath is a glorious area of about 790 acres of sweeping meadows, magical glades, mysterious crannies, ancient woodlands heathland and ponds. The ponds are used for swimming and fishing. It is an important refuge for wildlife, including muntjac deer, grass snakes, foxes, rabbits, slow worms, squirrels, terrapins, and frogs.

www.cityoflondon.gov.uk

Thrifty Tip
Hampstead Heath
Wild Swimming

Why not try wild swimming at Hampstead Heath Ponds.

The ponds are open daily and there are Men's and Women's ponds.
Admission Concessions £1 Adults £2
www.hampsteadheath.net

* Hyde Park London W2

Hyde Park in London has something for everyone. You can enjoy swimming, boating, cycling and skating. There are pitches for team games, tennis courts, tracks for horse riding and a spectacular children's playground. Other highlights of Hyde Park include the Italian Gardens, and the Rose Garden.
There is also a pet cemetery.
www.royalparks.org.uk/parks/hyde-park

* Hyde Park's Joy of Life Fountain
Diana Princess of Wales Memorial

This fountain, on the eastern edge of Hyde Park, forms part of the Diana Princess of Wales Memorial Walk. The Joy of Life fountain is a very popular spot for splashing around in the summer.

Interesting Fact
Hyde Park
Serpentine Swimmers

The Serpentine Swimming Club is an all year round open air swimming club, affiliated to the ASA. The main organisation of the club revolves around the Saturday morning handicap races, held at 8am throughout the year. The most famous race is the Peter Pan Cup, held every Christmas Day at 9am.

The Cup was originally awarded by JM Barrie himself see website for details.
www.serpentineswimmingclub.com

* Thrifty Tip
Hyde Park Serpentine Lido
Serpentine Lido is open spring/summer season from May through to September. As well as the 100m swimming area, there is a children's paddling pool, waterside tables, sun loungers and a cafe.
Admission Children £1 Concessions £3.00 Adult £4.00
www.royalparks.org.uk

* Hyde Park
Serpentine Boating Lake &
The Solar Shuttle
Rowing and pedal boats are available to hire on the Serpentine. The Solar shuttle travels between the Diana, Princess of Wales Memorial Fountain, which is on the south side of the Serpentine to the new Boat House on the northern edge of the lake near the newly-refurbished Dell restaurant.
www.royalparks.org.uk

Interesting Fact
Hyde Park
Hyde Park was used by William Friese-Greene for the first moving pictures.
www.royalparks.org.uk

Jubilee Park Canary Wharf London E14
A roof garden built above an underground station. The park sustains visual interest with raised elevations, and undulating lawns, wavy walls. The central feature is a raised serpentine water channel with rough stone walls.
www.canarywharf.com

* Thrifty Tip
FREE Summer Theatre at Jubilee Park
Enjoy a summer celebration at Canary Wharf of free outdoor family entertainment. With theatre performances especially designed for children and adults to enjoy together
See website:
www.canarywharf.com

Postmans Park London EC1
This tiny park within the Square Mile has a Victorian memorial to people who died while trying to save others (many complete strangers). The park was founded by Painter & Sculpter G F Watts to mark Queen Victoria's Jubilee.

Interesting Fact
GF Watts
GF Watts who was an outspoken socialist was known as England's Michaelangelo.

* Regents Park London NW1
The Regent's Park was designed by John Nash, covers 197 Hectares and includes excellent sports facilities spanning nearly 100 acres it includes the largest outdoor sports area in central London.

The park also has a short bird walk that guides you through the park describing the types of birds you are likely to encounter.
www.royalparks.org.uk

Interesting Facts
Regents Park
Regents Park Queen Mary's rose garden is London's largest collection of roses with approx 12,000 roses.

The Park also houses London Zoo, and The Open Air Theatre. Deck chairs are available for hire.

* Thrifty Tips
Regents Park
Boating Lake
The boating lake is open daily from 10:00 am to 6:00 pm from April through to September and offers rowing boats and adult pedalos for hire.
Early Bird Hire before 12pm from only £4

* Thrifty Tip
Regents Park Bandstands FREE Concerts
The Park has bandstands which hold a variety of FREE lunchtime and evening concerts see website for listings:
www.royalparks.org.uk

* Richmond Park London TW10
The park has a wide range of facilities on offer, including a children's playground at Petersham Gate.

Richmond Park, originally a deer-hunting park, still has 300 Red Deer and 350 fallow deer.

Interesting Facts
Richmond Park
The park also has over 70 pairs of Parakeets.

Ian Drury Musical Bench
To mark his life Ian's family have donated a bench (sponsored by Warner Chappell Music) to Richmond Park. It can be found at Poet's Corner within the grounds of Pembroke Lodge. Designer Mil Stricevic designed the 'talking park bench' as part of his Sonic Vista project to enable people to listen to the music of Ian Drury whilst enjoying views of the park.
www.royalparks.org.uk/parks

* St James Park London W1
St James's Park is the oldest Royal Park in London and is surrounded by three palaces. Facilities in the Park include a children's playground and deck chairs (April-September).

Interesting Fact
St James Park
The park also has a beautiful lake with Swans, Pelicans (a gift from Russia) and the odd Flamingo.
www.royalparks.org.uk/parks

Wimbledon Common
London SW19

Wimbledon Common has labyrinths of leafy glades, tangled thickets of wild red rose, bramble, and honeysuckle. The most prominent feature of the Common is the Wimbledon Windmill. Many events are held on the Common each year see website: **www.wpcc.org.uk**

Skate Parks

Skate Parks
London has several other very good skate parks to find one close visit the London Skate Park website:
www.londonskateparks.co.uk

* Skateboard Park Birdcage Walk
London SE1
The under croft of the Southbank Centre (Under the National Film Theatre) has pretty much been the heart of London skateboarding for around 40 plus years now. The area set aside for skateboarders comprises of a variety of ledges, banks and a set of stairs. Also a great place to see graffiti art.

Thrifty Tip Skating

* Easy Peasy Skate
FREE Group Skate
Battersea Park

The Easy Peasy Skate (no roads, no cars, and no hills) is a **FREE** group skate starting at 10:30am, every dry Saturday by the Japanese Peace Pagoda, Battersea Park.
www.easypeasyskate.com

Friday Night Skate Hyde Park
London Friday Night Skate and Sunday Stroll are weekly marshaled street skates in central London. The LFNS departs from Wellington Arch at Hyde Park Corner every Friday at 8pm.

Sunday Skate Hyde Park
The Sunday Stroll departs from Serpentine Road in Hyde Park every Sunday at 2pm. The events are open to all skaters able to stop, turn and control their speed on hills. They welcome both inline ('rollerblade') and quad ('roller skate') skaters. Children are welcome provided they're accompanied by a responsible adult.
www.lfns.co.uk

Skate Hire London
Skates can be hired in London from Slick Willies see website for prices and details:
www.slickwillies.co.uk

Woods

In springtime bluebells carpet the floors of all the beautiful woods below:

Bluebell Wood London N11

Bluebell Wood is a small area of ancient woodland covering just over one hectare located towards the eastern edge of Muswell Hill. The Wood is home to a variety of wildlife including the rare wild service tree. Birds including song thrush, chaffinch and magpie are commonly seen as well as butterflies and mammals such as squirrel, hedgehog and wood mouse.

www.haringey.gov.uk

Highgate Wood London N10

Highgate Wood is 28 hectares of ancient woodland predominantly an oak, hornbeam and holly wood. It is a haven for wildlife and provides numerous easily accessible and scenic woodland trails. .

www.cityoflondon.gov.uk/things-to-do/green-spaces/highgate-wood

Interesting Facts
Highgate Wood

The rich diversity of wildlife in Highgate Wood has been well researched and documented. To date over 900 invertebrate species, 338 moth species, 353 fungi species, 70 bird species and seven bat species have been recorded.

www.cityoflondon.gov.uk/things-to-do/green-spaces/highgate-wood

* Highgate Wood &
Queens Wood London N10

Queens Wood is close to Highgate Wood it is a hilly wood where nature goes crazy.

The wood has a popular miniature adventure playground. However the best fun can be had on the amazing hidden features the swings hidden in amongst the trees.

Isabella Plantation
(Bluebell Walk)
Richmond Park London
The Isabella Plantation is an ornamental woodland garden a real botanist's paradise. Full of exotic plants it is designed to be interesting all year round. Visitors can see camellias, magnolias, as well as daffodils and bluebells. From late April, the azaleas and rhododendrons are in flower.
www.royalparks.org.uk

Oxleas Wood
Greenwich London SE10
Oxleas Wood is very impressive ancient woodland dominated by tall oak trees, with hazel and sweet chestnut. It is reckoned by ecologists to be one of the most important woodlands for wildlife in the whole of London.

Section 4
Galleries &
Other Places to See Art

Section 4

Art Galleries

Gallery Lates FREE Events
Many London Galleries have late night openings with talks, music workshops food drink and more. Many of the evening Events are FREE see individual gallery websites for full details.

Children's Art Galleries

* Couper Collection Battersea Beach London SW11
The Couper Collection Museum of First Art shows artwork by young London artists from local schools.
Admission FREE
www.coupercollection.org.uk

London International Gallery of Children's Art
The online Gallery is devoted to encouraging the creativity of children and to promoting international understanding through cultural exchange. Their hope is to open the eyes of visitors to the integrity and power of children's art.
www.ligca.org

Contemporary/Modern Art Galleries

Aram Gallery London WC2
Independent curated space that promotes the
understanding of contemporary art and design.
www.thearamgallery.org

* Barbican Centre the Curve
London Silk Street EC2
The Barbican Centre has two art galleries the
main gallery, Barbican Art Gallery, and a smaller
space, The Curve. The Curve is a free
exhibition space for specially commissioned
works and contemporary art.
Admission FREE
www.barbican.org.uk

Belgravia Gallery Albemarle Street W1
This beautiful private gallery holds pieces by
HRH the Prince of Wales (Prince Charles),
Picasso, Andy Warhol, and Nelson Mandela
amongst others.
www.belgraviagallery.com

Café Gallery Southwark Park
London SE16
An artist led initiative providing exhibitions of
contemporary art in Southwark Park. Cafe
Gallery is a modern purpose built space
comprising three interlinked white room spaces
with a patio garden.
Admission FREE
www.cgplondon.org

Calvert22 Gallery London E2

Calvert 22 supports both emergent and more established artists through a carefully designed and contextualised programme of exhibitions and events, and aims to further illuminate their practice and context through original publications, related talks and events.

Admission FREE
www.calvert22.org

Interesting Fact
Calvert 22

The UK's only not for profit foundation dedicated to the presentation of contemporary art and culture from Russia, and Eastern Europe.

Thrifty Tip
Calvert 22
FREE Talks & Screenings

The Gallery hosts events including talks and screenings many of these are FREE to attend see website:
www.calvert22.org

* Camden Arts Centre
London NW3

Camden Arts Centre is a venue for contemporary visual art and education. Placing the artist at the core. Camden Arts Centre strives to involve members of the public in the ideas and processes of todays artists, and the artists who inspire them.

Admission FREE
www.camdenartscentre.org

* Camden Arts Centre
FREE Activities
FREE Art & Craft activates for families and children see website for listings.
www.camdenartscentre.org

Chisenhale Gallery
This Gallery has a 25-year history as one of London's most innovative organisations for contemporary visual art. See website for further details and opening times:
Admission FREE
www.chisenhale.org.uk

Institute of Contemporary Art
London SW1
The Institute of Contemporary Art Galleries are open during Exhibitions see website for current list:
Admission FREE
www.ica.org.uk

Kings Place Gallery London N1
Kings Place has two major commercial galleries Kings Place Gallery at gallery level, and Pangolin London near the entrance. Kings Place Gallery presents a programme of temporary and touring exhibitions by artists of national and international distinction. Pangolin London which is one of the few London galleries dedicated to exhibitions of modern and contemporary sculpture.
Admission FREE
www.kingsplace.co.uk/galleries

Louise Blouin Foundation London W11
The philosophy of the Foundation is
experimentation, questioning, debate, and
learning. They present the work of individual
artists through temporary exhibitions,
installations, performances and screenings.
Admission FREE
www.ltbfoundation.org

Orleans House Gallery Richmond
The Richmond upon Thames Borough Art
Collection was founded in 1962 with the
Ionides Bequest it has grown and developed to
comprise over 2,400 oil paintings, prints,
drawings, photographs and objects spanning the
early 18th century to the present day.
Admission FREE
www.richmond.gov.uk/orleans_house_galle
ry

*Thrifty Tip
Orleans House Gallery
FREE Arts & Crafts
FREE drop-in art & craft workshops for
families see website:
www.richmond.gov.uk

Pitzhanger Gallery
Ealing W5
The Gallery & House, Ealing's flagship cultural
venue, comprises of the Grade I listed
Pitzhanger Manor-House, designed by the
architect John Soane in 1800.

The Gallery is West London's premier professional contemporary arts venue.
Admission FREE
www.ealing.gov.uk

Pump House Gallery London W11
The gallery's programmer has engagement at its core and delivers a broad range of projects, exhibitions and activities. Collaboration is central to Pump House Gallery's programmer, working in partnership with curators, artists and organizations to bring engaging contemporary art to the public.
Admission FREE
www.pumphousegallery.org.uk

Interesting Fact
Pump House Gallery
Pump House Gallery is housed in a distinctive four story grade I listed Victorian tower.

Rivington Place Gallery London EC2
The Rivington Place Gallery's RIBA award-winning building is dedicated to the display debate and reflection of global diversity issues in the contemporary visual arts.
Admission FREE
www.rivingtonplace.org

Royal College of Music Portraits Dept
South Kensington SW7
At College Hall the Portraits and Performance History Collection houses a diverse collection relating to the history of performance.

This includes the RCM's internationally famous collection of images, comprising 340 original portraits and sculptures, and 25,000 prints and photographs.
Admission FREE
www.cph.rcm.ac.uk

Saatchi Gallery Chelsea SW3
The Saatchi Gallery is a gallery for contemporary art, opened by Charles Saatchi in 1985 in order to exhibit his collection to the public. Both Tracey Emin & Damien Hirst have exhibited at Saatchi Gallery.
Admission FREE to all exhibitions
www.saatchi-gallery.co.uk

Interesting Fact
Charles Saatchi
Charles Saatchi is known worldwide as an art collector, he is also known for his sponsorship of the Young British Artists (YBAs) including Damien Hirst and Tracey Emin.

Interesting Fact
Tracey Emin at
Saatchi Gallery
Tracey Emin's famous work "My Bed" was exhibited at Saatchi Gallery in 1998.

Interesting Fact
Tracey Emin
Tracey Emin designed a tube map cover for London Underground in 2012 why not see if you can pick up a copy.
www.art.tfl.gov.uk

Serpentine Gallery London W2
Serpentine Gallery is one of London's best-loved galleries for modern and contemporary art. The Gallery has a changing programme of exhibitions.
Admission FREE
www.serpentinegallery.org

Interesting Facts
Serpentine Gallery
In the grounds of the Gallery is a permanent work by artist and poet Ian Hamilton Finlay, dedicated to the Serpentine's former Patron Diana Princess of Wales.

The Pavilion Commission
The Serpentine's annual Pavilion commission is one of the most anticipated events on the cultural calendar, it is a program of temporary structures by internationally acclaimed architects and designers.

The Pavilion 2013 was designed by multi award-winning Japanese architect Sou Fujimoto.

Thrifty Tip
Serpentine Gallery
FREE Talks
FREE talks and seminars (sometimes by prominent artists) on Saturdays at 3pm explore themes related to the current work on show.
www.serpentinegallery.org

South London Gallery
London SE5

The South London Gallery has an international reputation for its programmer of contemporary art exhibitions and live art events, with integrated education projects for children, young people and adults.
Admission FREE
www.southlondongallery.org

* Thrifty Tip
South London Gallery
FREE Workshops
FREE drop-in workshops for children and families during school holidays are themed around current exhibitions and are open to all.
www.southlondongallery.org

Subway Gallery London W2
The gallery opened in June 2006 and it is situated below Edgware Rd/Harrow Rd crossing in a W2 pedestrian subway. Conceived by artist Robert Gordon McHarg III, the space is a 1960's kiosk with glass walls which creates a unique showcase for art.
Admission FREE
www.subwaygallery.com

The Hayward Gallery
Southbank Centre
London SE1
The gallery is part of the Southbank Centre complex; it is one of London's most important spaces for contemporary art.
Admission FREE to some exhibitions
www.haywardgallery.org.uk

Interesting Fact
The Hayward Gallery
The Hayward Gallery is named after Sir Isaac Hayward a former leader of the London County Council.

The Mall Galleries London
The Mall Galleries champion new contemporary figurative art by living artist. The Mall Galleries is also the home of the Federation of British Artists.
Admission FREE
www.mallgalleries.org.uk

The Tate Modern
London SE1
The Tate Modern is an institution that houses International Modern and Contemporary Art. The permanent collection includes work by Miro, Monet, Picasso, Jackson Pollock and more. They also have a programmer of exhibitions.
Admission FREE
www.tate.org.uk

Interesting Fact
The Tate Modern
The galleries are housed in the former Bankside Power Station, which was originally designed by Sir Giles Gilbert Scott.
www.tate.org.uk

Victoria Miro
London N1

Victoria Miro Gallery represents established names such as film and installation artist Doug Aitken, and younger talent including Conrad Shawcross. The gallery has a beautiful landscaped area overlooking a stretch of the Regent's Canal at Wenlock Basin which has been used to great effect for installations.
Admission FREE
www.victoria-miro.com

Interesting Fact
Victoria Miro
The gallery represents two winners of the Turner Prize Chris Ofili, who won the prize in 1998 and the 2003 winner Grayson Perry.

White Cubicle
George & Dragon London E2
The White Cubicle Toilet Gallery is located within the Ladies Toilet of the George and Dragon, and works with no budget, staff or boundaries. Since 2005 White Cubicle has been presenting a discerning programme of local and international manifestations as an antidote to London's art scene.
www.whitecubicle.org

Cutural Art Galleries

Ben Uri Gallery London NW8
The Ben Uri Collection is the world's most distinguished body of work by artists of European Jewish descent.

You can now see around a third of Ben Uri's 1300 artworks in the Collection.
Admission Concessions £4 Adults £5
www.benuri.org.uk

Brunei Gallery at
School of Oriental and African Studies
London WC1
The Brunei Gallery is an exciting venue in central London that hosts a programme of changing contemporary and historical exhibitions from Asia, Africa and the Middle East.
Admission FREE
www.soas.ac.uk

Interesting Fact
School of Oriental and African Studies
Among the wealth of material are illustrated Islamic manuscripts, a 16th century book of animal fables; Chinese and Japanese paintings and prints; varied ceramic objects from the Middle East.

The Estorick Collection of
Modern Italian Art
London N1
The Estorick Collection includes Picasso, Gris, and Leger is also known internationally for its core of Futurist works.
Admission Concessions £3.50 Adults £5
Admission FREE to Children and Students
www.estorickcollection.com

**The Flemming Scottish Art Gallery
London W1**
The Fleming Collection is the finest collection
of Scottish art in private hands. The collection
comprises over 750 oils and watercolours from
1770 to the present day. These include works by
Raeburn, Ramsay, Wilkie and the iconic
paintings of the Highland Clearances.
**Admission FREE
www.flemingcollection.co.uk**

Goeth Institute London SW7
The Goethe Institute is the cultural institute of
the Federal Republic of Germany with a global
reach. They also provide information on
Germany's cultural, social and political life. To
view a list of exhibitions see the website:
**Admission FREE
www.goethe.de/ins/gb/lon**

**Thrifty Tip
Goeth Institute**
FREE Events throughout the year including
film screenings

**The Harold Samuel Art Collection
Mansion House London EC4**
The ASAC is a unique collection of 17th
century paintings from Holland's Golden Age.
The collection was bequeathed to the City of
London in 1987 by Lord Harold Samuel a
wealthy property developer and entrepreneur.
Tours are every Tuesday at 2pm Concessions
£5 Adults £7 see website for full details.
www.cityoflondon.gov.uk

Thrifty Tip
Mansion House
Admission FREE
During Open House Weekend
The Mansion House participates in Open
House where you can visit for FREE. The next
Open House will takes place in **September.**
www.londonopenhouse.org

Spanish Institute London SW1
The Spanish Institute promotes knowledge of
the Spanish language abroad and foster
international cultural cooperation, they also
provide information on Spain's cultural life. To
view a list of exhibitions see the website:
www.londres.cervantes.es

Italian Cultural Institute London SW1
The Cultural Institutes promote the image of
Italy as centre of production, conservation and
diffusion of culture from the Classical age to
nowadays.
To view a list of exhibitions see the website:
www.icilondon.esteri.it/IIC_Londra

Indian Office Collection
British Library London NW1
The British Library's collection of prints,
drawings and photographs from the Indian
subcontinent and its surrounding territories is
one of the world's greatest visual records of the
cultural history of South Asia from the late-18th
to the mid-20th century.
Admission FREE
www.bl.uk

Floating Art Galleries

Cascade Floating Art Gallery
Regents Canal
A former historic barge on Regents Canal, the barge is now home to the Cascade Art. **Gallery.**
0207 289 7050

The Couper Collection
Battersea Beach SW11
The Couper Collection exhibits artwork and installations by London artist Max Couper made onboard a fleet of historic Thames barges over the past two decades. The programme is made up of live events, new artist's exhibitions, discussions, educational collaborations, and ecology.
Admission FREE
www.coupercollection.org.uk

Interesting Fact
The Couper Collection
The Couper Collection is London's last remaining fleet of historic Thames barges on their ancient moorings.

Art Galleries Other

* Interesting Fact
Artsline
Artsline is a disabled led Charity established in 1981 to promote access for disabled people to arts and entertainment venues promoting the clear message that access equals inclusion.

Artsline has set up an online website of approved accessible arts and entertainment venues visit their website to view. **www.artsline.org.uk**

* Animation Art Gallery
Marylebone London W1

The Animation Art Gallery displays a range of animation, sculpture and illustrations from popular culture and television programmers, such as The Simpsons, Thunderbirds and Wallace and Gromit.
Admission FREE
www.animationartgallery.com

Centre for Recent Drawing
Islington London N1

The Centre for Recent Drawing is London's museum space for drawing. Since 2004 CRD has provided a public exhibition space and exhibition series that is independent and non-commercial, and is a member of the Museum Association of the UK.
Check website for current exhibitions.
Admission is FREE
www.c4rd.org.uk

Courtauld Institute of Art
London WC2

One of the world's leading centers for the study of the history and conservation of art and architecture. Its Gallery houses one of Britain's best-loved collections. Based at Somerset House.

Admission **FREE** (Under 18s Students &
Teachers and the Unemployed)
**Admission £3 on Mondays from 10am until
2pm**
www.courtauld.ac.uk

* Dulwich Picture Gallery London SE21
Sir Francis Bourgeois RA bequeathed his
collection of old masters for the inspection of
the public. The Collection includes Rembrandt,
Rubens, Poussin, Murillo, and Gainsborough,
amongst others.
Admission Senior citizens £4.00 Adults £5.00
Admission FREE (for unemployed, disabled,
children and students).
www.dulwichpicturegallery.org.uk

Interesting Fact
Dulwich Picture Gallery
DPG was England's first public art gallery it
was founded in 1811 and was designed by John
Soanes.

Interesting Fact
Sir John Soanes
If you like Soanes work, or indeed art & design
then a visit to the Soane Museum is a must. The
architect John Soane designed the house to live
in, but also as a setting for his antiquities and his
works of art. The collections include over 250
historical architectural models including
examples of furniture and decorative art. There
are also paintings by Hogarth and Caneletto.
Admission FREE
www.soane.org

*** Foundling Museum Art Collection
London WC1**
William Hogarth (1697-1764) devoted over
twenty-five years of his life to the Foundling
Hospital, becoming the leading artistic
contributor to the Foundling Hospital Art
Collection. Hogarth donated paintings and
encouraged his contemporaries to do the same
leading to the creation of the Foundling
Hospital Art Collection.
Admission Concession £5 Adults £7.50
Admission FREE (Children up to 16 years)
www.foundlingmuseum.org.uk

*** Interesting Facts
Foundling Museum**
Artist Grayson Perry is a Foundling Fellow, the
Foundling Fellows work with the museum to
develop creative initiatives for children.

**Foundling Museum
Handel Collection Research Library**
The composer George Frederic Handel was a
Governor and benefactor of the Foundling
Hospital. In addition to the score and parts of
Messiah the Museum holds the Gerald Coke
Handel Collection, an important Collection of
material relating to Handel and his
contemporaries.
See website for viewing details.
www.foundlingmuseum.org.uk

Hogarth House Chiswick London W4
Hogarth House was the country home of the
great painter William Hogarth.

Hogarth's talents and interests were wide-ranging, and displays in the house tell the story of his life at the house. Several of Hogarth's paintings are on view.
Admission FREE
www.hounslow.info

Interesting Fact
William Hogarth
The English Painter & Printmaker William Hogarth was a patron of the Foundling Museum.

*Guildhall Gallery London EC2
The Gallery shows a changing display of about 250 artworks from its collection of paintings, drawings and sculpture, in addition to a program of temporary exhibitions.
Admission FREE
www.guildhall.cityoflondon.gov.uk

* Interesting Fact
Guildhall Gallery Amphitheatre
The Museum of London Archaeological Service discovered the remains of London's Roman Amphitheatre in the Guildhall Gallery building. The building was re-designed to incorporate this astounding piece of architectural history.
www.cityoflondon.gov.uk

Flaxman Gallery
UCL
London WC1
UCL Art Museum has an unrivalled collection of works by the Neo-classical sculptor John Flaxman.

Flaxman was known throughout Europe for his innovative drawing style and for his sculptures, and University College possesses many examples of works in both these media.
Admission FREE
www.ucl.ac.uk/museums

Fulham Palace Gallery
London SW6
The beautiful gallery rooms at Fulham Palace are open from Saturday to Wednesday from 1pm - 4pm, when an art exhibition is taking place see website for details:
Admission FREE
www.fulhampalace.org

Guardian News & Media Gallery
Kings X London N1
The Guardian News and Media gallery has a rolling programme of exhibitions which investigate and reflect upon aspects of news and newspapers and the role of journalism. The programme draws heavily on the archive collections.
Admission FREE
www.kingsplace.co.uk/galleries

* Kenwood House Hampstead
London NW3
This Stunning neo-classical villa on the edge of Hampstead Heath was designed by Robert Adam.

The house has a permanent exhibition of an outstanding collection of paintings including a Rembrandt self-portrait, Botticelli and Vermeer, etc the house also has a collection of other art objects. The garden has sculptures by Sir Henry Moore, and a beautiful lake.

Admission FREE

www.english-heritage.org.uk/daysout/properties/kenwood-house

* National Gallery Trafalgar Square WC2

The National Gallery houses the national collection of Western European painting from the 13th to the 19th centuries. With **FREE** access to over 2,300 paintings from da Vinci to van Gogh, there's something for everyone at the National Gallery.

Admission FREE

www.nationalgallery.org.uk

Thrifty Tips
National Gallery Quick Talks

Get a quick insight into one painting with a 10-minute talk at the National Gallery, from Friday to Tuesday at 4pm.

National Gallery
In Depth Talks

Every month they have a range of free talks explore wider themes in the collection at their in-depth theatre talks.

www.nationalgallery.org.uk

Interesting Fact
Outside the National Gallery
Sitting on the steps below the National Gallery
are the imperial Measures.

* National Gallery
Family Sundays FREE Workshops
The Sunday workshops at the National Gallery
are free and include Art Workshops, Magic
Carpet Storytelling, and family Walk & Talk.

* National Portrait Gallery London WC2
Houses a collection of portraits of historically
important and famous British people. It was
the first portrait gallery in the world when it
opened in 1856.
Admission FREE
www.npg.org.uk

Interesting Fact
National Portrait Gallery
Late Shift in partnership with FTI Consulting
offers new ways to explore the Gallery after
hours and socialise after work. Enjoy a wide
range of events including art talks.

Orleans House Gallery Richmond
The main gallery hosts five temporary
exhibitions each year. Ranging from the
historical to the contemporary. The Gallery
attracts over 56,000 visitors annually.
Admission FREE
www.richmond.gov.uk

* Thrifty Tip
Orleans House FREE Arts & Crafts
FREE drop-in arts and crafts workshops for
families, 2pm - 3:30pm, no booking necessary
see website for details.

Pump House Gallery Battersea SW11
Pump House Gallery is a public contemporary
exhibition space housed in a distinctive four
story grade I listed Victorian tower, on the
lakeside in Battersea Park, South London.
Admission FREE
www.pumphousegallery.org.uk

Royal Academy of Arts London W1
The Royal Academy of Arts is a privately
funded institution led by eminent artists and
architects. The collection focuses on British art
and artists and predominantly ranges from the
18th century to the present day.
Highlights Include major works by Reynolds,
Gainsborough, Turner, Constable, Alma-
Tadema, Flaxman, Millais, Leighton,
Waterhouse, Sargent, Spencer and Hockney.
Admission Children12-18 years/unwaged £4
Students £9
www.royalacademy.org.uk

Interesting Fact
Royal Academy of Arts
Summer Exhibition
The Academy has held an annual Summer
Exhibition of works for sale since its formation.

An artist can enter a maximum of two works
for a handling charge of £25 per work. To find

out more about RA or the summer exhibition
see the website:
www.royalacademy.org.uk

* Royal Academy of Arts
FREE Workshops
FREE drop in workshops for children and
families at the RA Learning Studio - see website.
www.royalacademy.org.uk

Interesting Fact
Burlington House
Arts & Sciences W1
Burlington House as well as being home to
Royal Academy of Arts it is also home to the
Society of Antiquaries, Linnean Society,
Geological Society, Royal Astronomical Society
and the Royal Society of Chemistry.

* Interesting Fact
Burlington House Fountains
The layout of the fountains in the central
Annenberg Courtyard was created in 2000 and
reflects the pattern of the planets in relation to
the stars at the birth of Sir Joshua Reynolds (the
first president of the Royal Academy) 16 July
1723.
www.burlingtonhouse.org

Thrifty Tip
Burlington House
FREE Lectures and Events

Burlington House has a programme of public lectures and events that allows everyone to access the exciting scientific and artistic output of the societies.
Admission FREE
www.burlingtonhouse.org

Royal College of Art
Kensington London SW7
The RCA's galleries and lecture theatres are home to a lively programme of exhibitions, events and talks. They regularly present work by postgraduate students and lectures by leading art and design figures.
Admission FREE (unless otherwise stated)
www.rca.ac.uk

Slade School of Fine Art London WC1
Slade students and staff initiate and engage in a wide range of events and projects. Some of these are hosted by the Slade such as the annual Degree Shows and Graduate Interim Show which takes place late May and early June you can visit during this time.
Admission FREE
www.ucl.ac.uk/slade

* St Paul's Cathedral
Arts Project
London EC4
The St Paul's Cathedral Arts Project is an ongoing programmer which seeks to explore the encounter between art and faith.

Projects have included installations by Anthony Gormley, Rebecca Horn, Yoko Ono and Martin Firrell see website:
www.stpauls.co.uk/Cathedral-History/Arts-Programme

Temple Gallery London W11
Opened by Richard Temple this gallery has an amazing display of ancient icons and religious art. Including a collection of Byzantine, Greek, Cretan and Russian Icons
This is a commercial Gallery.
www.templegallery.com

Interesting Fact
Temple Gallery
The gallery has helped several major museums acquire icons.

* The Kennel Club Art Gallery London W1
The Kennel Club Art Gallery houses the largest collection of dog paintings in Europe. The collection features works by famous dog artists.
www.thekennelclub.org.uk/artgallery

* The Tate
London SW1
The Tate holds the national collection of British art from 1500 to the present day and international modern and contemporary art. The collection includes nearly 70,000 artworks by over 3,000 artists and grows every year.

With over 2000 artworks by Joseph Mallord William Turner.
Admission FREE
www.tate.org.uk

Interesting Fact
The Tate
The gallery was founded in 1897 and was originally named the National Gallery of British Art. In 1932 it was renamed the Tate Gallery after sugar magnate Henry Tate (son of a clergyman) of Tate & Lyle who had laid the foundations for the collection.

The Topoloski Century South Bank SE1
The Gallery presents a large artwork by Feliks Topolski (1907–1989), located in the Hungerford Bridge arches. It presents a panoramic view of key events and people in the 20th century. The installation forms a mural that is 600 feet long.
Admission £2
www.topolskicentury.org.uk

Thrifty Tip
The Topoloski Century
50 plus Workshops
Open to everyone over 50 every weekday afternoons from 2- 4pm with tea and biscuits cost £5.
www.topolskicentury.org.uk

UCL Art Museum
London WC1
Over 10,000 works of art make up the collections of UCL Art Museum from the 1500s

to the present day. Works separated by centuries are linked by a desire to experiment with new materials and reproduction techniques in order to produce new meanings to share ideas and inspire.
Admission FREE
www.ucl.ac.uk/museums

Wallace Collection London W1
The Wallace Collection is a national museum in an historic London town house. In 25 galleries are unsurpassed displays of French 18th century painting, furniture and porcelain with superb Old Master paintings and a world class armoury.
Admission FREE
www.wallacecollection.org

Whitechapel Gallery London E1
Whitechapel Gallery has premiered world-class artists from modern masters such as Pablo Picasso, Jackson Pollock, to contemporaries such as Sophie Calle, Lucian Freud, and Gilbert & George. With beautiful galleries, exhibitions, artist commissions, collection displays, historic archives, education resources, and inspiring art courses.
Admission FREE
www.whitechapelgallery.org

White Cube Bermondsey London SE1
Designed by Casper Mueller Kneer Architects who are based in London and Berlin. The building includes three principal exhibition spaces.

See website for current exhibitions:
Admission FREE.
www.whitecube.com

Thrifty Tip
White Cube
FREE Events &
FREE Film Screenings
White Cube have several FREE events
including FREE Sunday Film Screenings see
website for listings:
www.whitecube.com

White Cube Hoxton London N1
White Cube Hoxton Square was set up as a
second gallery space in London's East End.
Housed in a 1920s light industrial building
White Cube Hoxton Square has 2000 square
feet of uninterrupted exhibition space.
Admission FREE
www.whitecube.com

Other Places to See Amazing Art

Denis Severs House London E1
A Grade II listed Georgian terraced house in
Spitalfields From 1979 to 1999 it was lived in by
Dennis Severs a Canadian Artist, who gradually
recreated the rooms as a time capsule in the
style of former centuries mainly from the 18th
and 19th centuries. A must visit for anyone
who loves Art & Design.
www.dennissevershouse.co.uk

Thrifty Tip
Denis Severs House
Visit on Mondays Lunchtimes between 12pm-2pm for just £7.
www.dennissevershouse.co.uk

* Museum of Instruments London SW7
The Museum has significant portraits from the RCM collection, including oil paintings of Haydn, Boyce and Farinelli, as well as manuscripts, early printed edition, photographs, letters and many other objects.
Admission FREE
www.rcm.ac.uk/visit/museum

Royal Academy of Music London NW1
Alongside these are some of the most significant portraits from the RCM collection, including oil paintings of Haydn, Boyce & Farinelli, as well as manuscripts, early printed edition, photographs, letters and many other objects from the Library and Special Collections.
Admission FREE
www.rcm.ac.uk/visit/museum

Interesting Fact
Royal Academy of Music
Mezzo-Soprano Katherine Jenkins and Singer Songwriter Elton John were students at RAM.
www.rcm.ac.uk/visit/museum

Victoria & Albert Museum
Paintings Collection London SW7

The V&A Paintings collection which includes superlative holdings of British watercolours and portrait miniatures as well as over 2,000 British and European oil paintings.
Admission FREE
www.vam.ac.uk

Thrifty Tip
Victoria & Albert Museum
British Galleries Tour Join this daily one hour tour which introduces the V&A's stunning British Galleries which house the most comprehensive collection of British art and design on view anywhere in the world.
www.vam.ac.uk

Photographic Galleries

Getty Images London W1
Getty invites you to experience some of the greatest exhibitions, photographic galleries & collections that London has to offer. Their collections include millions of prints, negatives & transparencies from the 1850's to modern day masterpieces.
Admission FREE
www.gettyimagesgallery.com

Foto8 Gallery London EC1
Foto8 Gallery holds exhibitions and installations on Honduras Street and Photography in the main gallery see website for listings.
Admission FREE
www.foto8.com

Island History Trust
London E14
The people on the Isle of Dogs started
collecting photographs and reminiscence in
1981 this collection has become the Island
History Trust; telling the story of the Island
the docks and local life. Visit by appointment.
Admission FREE
www.islandhistory.org.uk

National Gallery Trafalgar Square
London WC2
The National Gallery sometimes has
photography exhibitions see website for details:
www.nationalgallery.org.uk

Photographers Gallery London W1
The Photographers' Gallery is the largest public
gallery in London dedicated to photography.
From the latest emerging talent, to historical
archives and established artists it is the place to
see photography.
Admission FREE except for special events
www.thephotographersgallery.org.uk

Proud Gallery
Camden NW1 & Chelsea London SW3
Over the last ten years Proud Galleries has
become Europe's most popular privately
funded photographic gallery. With a focus on
photography reflecting popular culture. With
rock & roll, fashion, sporting moments
and more.
Admission FREE
www.proudonline.co.uk

Victoria & Albert Museum
Photographers Gallery London SW7
V&A's new Photographs Gallery has an
inaugural display of works by key figures of
photographic history. The Photographs Gallery
draws upon the V&A's internationally
renowned collection of photographs, and
chronicles the history of photography.
Admission FREE
www.vam.ac.uk

Art Other

National Art Library
The National Art Library is a major public
reference library of fine and decorative arts of
many countries and periods. It is open to the
public as a reference library. Before you can use
the Library you must register as a Reader. This
can be done online in advance.
Admission FREE
**www.vam.ac.uk/page/n/national-art-
library**

Street Art

London has some amazing street art from
Banksy to Ray Walker there really is something
for everyone. Some of the most popular are
listed below to find out where you can see more
visit the London Mural Preservation Society
website:
www.londonmuralpreservationsociety.com

Battersea in Perspective
Dagnall Road and Culvert Street SW11
Painted in 1988 by Barnes Battersea comes
under his scrutiny, from an aerial perspective.
The plaque reveals just how many distinguished
aviators came from the area.

Brick Lane London E1
Brick lane has a reputation for it's art
exhibitions, and It's famous for graffiti and
street art it features work by Banksy, D*Face,
and Ben Eine.
www.visitbricklane.org

Brixton Academy Mural
Stockwell Park Road London SW9
This mural entitled "Children at Play" was
painted by artist Stephen Puscy, who was
approached by Lambeth council. The mural can
be seen on the wall of the fly-tower of Brixton
Academy, and is one of London's biggest
murals.

Brixton Railway Station
Market Mural
On the back wall of the station there are two
murals displaying the sort of wares you could
buy in Brixton market 25 years ago. These
murals were painted in 1986 as part of the
station's refurbishment.
The artists who worked on both pieces are
Karen Smith and Angie Biltcliffe from Anchor
Designs.

Camden Lock London NW1
Grafitti Wall Paper Hanging this piece by
famous British street artist Banksy can be seen
by the canal on the opposite side to the path.
Aristoc Rat and Fisher Boy also by Banksy can
also be seen by the canal on the opposite side to
the path.
www.banksy.co.uk

**Calthorpe Community Gardens
Murals & Mosaics London WC1**
The Calthorpe project is a quiet oasis set off
Grays Inn road, Kings Cross. It is also full of
home grown public art. Mosaics, murals and
sculptures are interwoven with the gardens.

*** Thrifty Tip
Calthorpe Community Gardens
FREE Activities**
Many FREE activities take place in the Gardens
throughout the year including Fetes, Garden
Parties, and a FREE parent Gym see website:
www.calthorpeproject.org.uk

Chumleigh Gardens London SE5
The Circle of Life in the pavement at
Chumleigh Gate was completed by Sue
Pritchard in Summer 2000 and has attracted
many visitors.

*** Interesting Fact
Chumleigh Gardens
Art in the Park**
Art in the Park is a charity devoted to enriching
Londoners' lives and environment through
making visual arts.

When visiting you may well see artists working in the park during your visit see Art in the Park website:
www.artinthepark.co.uk

Thrifty Tip
Chumleigh Gardens
Open Garden Squares Weekend
Chumleigh Gardens takes part in Open Garden Squares Weekend. Activities include a plant sale, artistic treasure hunt, live music, photographic exhibition, art workshops and some gardening/horticultural activities. The café will be serving cream teas in the gardens. See Open Squares website:
www.opensquares.org

Cromer Street Mosaics
Kings X London N1
Wander along Kings Cross's Cromer Street and you will find a large church dominating the road. Around the back of the building, you will find a little locked garden with 4 mosaic panels. These beautiful pieces were created by Diana Leary and Dave Bangs.

Cable Street Mural London E1
The Battle of Cable Street took place on Sunday 4 October 1936 in the East End of London. It was a clash between the Metropolitan Police and the British Union of Fascists, led by Oswald Mosley. The Battle is remembered in this staggering mural from 1993.

Fitzrovia Mural
Whitfield Gardens London W1
This memorial to the characters of Fitzrovia,
painted in 1980 by Mick Jones and Simon
Barber is one of London's best known murals.

Hertford Canal Tower Hamlet E3
Hot spot for Graffiti and street art, Banksy's
Baby with Blocks can be seen here.

Alfred Hitchcock Mosaics
Leytonstone Tube Station
Alfred Hitchcock was born at 517 High Road,
Leytonstone on 13 August 1899. To mark 100
years since this event, and to commemorate the
director's link with the area, 17 mosaics
dedicated to Hitchcock and his films have been
installed in the underpass at Leytonstone tube
station.

Magpie Alley Murals London EC4
Magpie Alley Just off Bouviere Street London
has a lovely display charting the history of
printing in the area.

Ode to the West Wind
Poland Street and Noel Street London W1
This corner of Soho is energised by a rather
surreal mural by Louise Vines. A large piece of
tree splits away and a man with a book looks
on.

Ray Walkers Mural
Dalston Lane London E8

The mural created by Ray Walker is a composition based on the 1983 Hackney Peace Carnival. In the picture, the procession has just gone past Navarino Mansions on Dalston Lane. A brass band plays at the front of the as people watch them go by.

Stockwell Memorial Mural Stockwell Roundabout SW9
The mural includes a picture of James Bond (Roger Moore who played Bond grew up in Stockwell). Artist, Vincent Van Gogh is included as he spent six months living in the area. A tube train also features as Stockwell is one of the earliest London tube stations. There is also a tribute to local resident and war hero Violette Szabo.

Interesting Fact
Violette Szabo
Lieutenant Violette Szabó, George Cross, Croix de Guerre with Star, Médaille de la Résistance, was a renowned undercover secret agent for Special Operations Executive in occupied France during the Second World War.
www.violetteszabo.org

The Spirit of Soho
Corner of Carnaby Street W1
This 1991 mural from the Free Form Arts Trust centres on St Anne dedicatee of the local church. Her gaudy frock contains a veritable A-Z of Soho.

Tottenham Court Road
Underground Station London W1
The Station has beautiful mosaics by British
Pop Artist Eduardo Paolozzi.

Window Display Art
If you love Art & Design do not miss London's
store displays our favourites include Fortnum &
Mason, Harvey Nichols Harrods, Liberty,
Selfridges and Tiffany.

Art Family Workshops

Art & Crafts Workshops for Families
See More Thrifty Tips Section of this book
Page 257

Section 5
Libraries & Museums

Section 5
Libraries & Museums

Libraries

British Library
Euston Road London NW1

The British Library is the national library of the UK and is the world's largest library in terms of total number of items. The library is a major research library. Many books and manuscripts are on display to the general public in the Sir John Ritblat Gallery which is open seven days a week at no charge.
Admission FREE
www.bl.uk

Interesting Facts
British Library

Also on display in this iconic building are some of the world's most famous written and printed items, such as the Magna Carta (1215) and Shakespeare's First Folio. Music treasures on display include Mendlessohns Wedding March. There is also a collection of Beetles lyrics that include Help, Ticket to Ride, and Yesterday.
www.bl.uk

Music Library

Original manuscripts of Alan Bush's compositions have been deposited at the British Library.
www.bl.uk

British Museum The Kings Library
London WC1

The King's Library was a royal collection of books created by King George III and donated to the nation. A gallery, named after the collection, was built at the British Museum in 1827 to house them.
Admission FREE
www.britishmuseum.org

Clockmakers Library & Museum
Fore Street London EC2
The Clockmakers' Museum collection is housed in the Guildhall Library and is the oldest collection specifically of clocks and watches in the world, with about 1,000 exhibits.
Admission FREE
www.cityoflondon.gov.uk

Estorick Collection of
Modern Italian Art Library
London N1
The Estorick Collection of Modern Italian Art has an art library. The Collection is known internationally for its core of Futurist works.
Admission Concessions £3.50 Adults £5.00
Admission FREE to Children and Students
www.estorickcollection.com

Guildhall Library Collection
London EC2
Guildhall Library is a public reference library which specialises in the history of London. The Library's printed books collection comprises over 200,000 titles dating from the 15th to the 21st centuries.

Admission FREE

Thrifty Tip
Guildhall Library Collection
Special collections at Guildhall library include
those devoted to Samuel Pepys, John Wilkes
and Thomas More, plus the libraries of the
Clockmakers', Gardeners' and Fletchers'
Companies, the Antiquarian Horological
Society, Gresham College, and the Charles
Lamb Society.

Handel Collection Research Library
Foundling Museum
The Collection of manuscripts, printed books
and music, paintings and engravings,
memorabilia, art works and ephemera, includes
Handel's will amongst its treasures.   In addition
to the public exhibition room open during
normal Museum hours, The Gerald Coke
Handel Research Library is open Wednesday-
Friday for research purposes by appointment.
www.foundlingmuseum.org.uk

Lambeth Palace Library
London SE1
Founded in 1610, the Library is one of
England's oldest public libraries, and has had a
rich and varied history. Amongst its treasures
are Charles 1's gloves worn just before his
execution, and a first edition of Sir Thomas
Mores Utopia.
www.lambethpalacelibrary.org

*** London Transport Museum Library
Covent Garden WC2**
The Library is open to anyone interested in
finding out more about London's public
transport - past, present and future. Opening
times are by appointment see website:
Admission FREE
www.ltmuseum.co.uk/visit/library

**Materials Library
Institute of Making London WC2**
At the heart of the Institute of Making is the
Materials Library –a repository of some of the
most extraordinary materials on earth, gathered
together not only for scientific interest, but also
for their ability to fire the imagination.

Please Note:
This is currently a time of transition for the
Institute of Making check website for opening
details:
www.materialslibrary.org.uk

**Marx Memorial Library
London EC1**
The aim of the Marx Memorial Library is
education, knowledge and learning by the
provision of a library of books, periodicals and
manuscripts relating to all aspects of the science
of Marxism. Also the history of Socialism and
the working class movement.
Admission FREE
www.marx-memorial-library.org

Interesting Fact
Karl Marx
Karl Marx is buried at Highgate Cemetery
See website for details:
www.highgatecemetery.org

National Art Library
V&A
London SW7
The National Art Library is a major public
reference library of fine and decorative arts of
many countries and periods. It is open to the
public as a reference library. Before you can use
the Library you must register as a Reader. This
can be done online in advance.
www.vam.ac.uk/page/n/national-art-library

Oriental Manuscript & Book Collection
London WC1
Here you can consult archives, manuscripts,
photographs, maps, audio-visual material and
rare books relating to Africa, Asia, the Middle
East, Europe, the Americas, the Caribbean, the
South Pacific and Australasia.
Admission FREE
www.soas.ac.uk/library/archives

Royal Academy of Music Library
London NW1
The RCM collection includes oil paintings as
well as manuscripts, early printed edition
photographs, letters and many other objects
from the Library and Special Collections.
Admission FREE
www.rcm.ac.uk/visit/museum

Rudolph Steiner House Library
London NW1
The Anthroposophical Society is based at Rudolf Steiner House and is part of the General Anthroposophical Society founded by Rudolf Steiner.Membership of the Library is open to everyone, see website for details:
Admission FREE
www.rsh.anth.org.uk

Thrifty Tip
Rudolph Steiner House
Rudolf Steiner gave many insights to help us to get to grips with the world we live in and to equip us to meet what is coming towards us. The Tuesday & Friday lecture series at RSH looks at aspects of these insights.
Concessions £1 Adults £3.50 see website for full details
www.rsh.anth.org.uk

St Brides Church Foundation Library
London EC4
St Brides Library is a wonderful resource for everyone it has over 50000 books in subjects ranging from graphic design, history of the book and journalism to social and economic history.
Tel: 0207 427 0133

The (Saison)
Poetry Library
Royal Festival Hall London SE1
The most comprehensive and accessible collection of poetry from 1912 in Britain.

It is the major library for modern and contemporary poetry. Poetry is available in many formats: books, pamphlets, audio cassette, CD, video and DVD for reference and loan; magazines, press cuttings, photographs, posters and postcards for reference.
Admission FREE
www.poetrylibrary.org.uk

Interesting Fact
The (Saison) Poetry Library
The Saison Poetry Library houses the Arts Council poetry collection, the most comprehensive and accessible collection of modern poetry in Britain.

The Wiener Library London WC1
The Wiener Library is the world's oldest Holocaust memorial institution. Set up by Alfred Wiener and Prof. David Cohen, the library has information about historical events in Nazi Germany.
Admission FREE
www.wienerlibrary.co.uk

The Women's Library
London E1
The Women's Library exists to document and explore the past, present and future lives of women in Britain. It houses the most extensive resource for women's history in the UK.
Admission FREE
www.londonmet.ac.uk/thewomenslibrary

Tyburn Convent Spiritual Library
London W1
Tyburn Convent is a monastery which has a
spiritual library.
Admission FREE
www.tyburnconvent.org.uk

Vaughan Williams Library
Cecil Sharp House London NW1
England's national folk music and dance
archive, a one stop shop for anybody interested
in the folk arts, with material on traditional
song, dance and music in the country.
Admission FREE
www.efdss.org

Thrifty Tips for Book Lovers

Booktrust
Book trust events take place up and down the
country to inspire people of all ages to get more
involved with reading and writing.
To find FREE Events in your area visit the
website:
www.booktrust.org.uk

Carnaby FREE Book Exchange
London W1
The Carnaby Book Exchange is a space where
you can pick up a book, relax in an armchair
and explore the vast expanses of fashion, travel,
music, photography, design and history, to
name but a few topics.

You are able to leave a book that you have read, and in return take one away from the space for FREE.
Check website for opening:
www.carnaby.co.uk

Daunt Bookshop
Hampstead London NW3
Free walking book group meets every last Sunday of the month at 11.30 on Hampstead Heath.
www.dauntbooks.co.uk

Floating Book Shop
London Canals
Word on the Water
London's only floating second-hand bookshop travels between Camden Lock, Angel, Hackney and Paddington stopping for two weeks at each mooring to sell books donated by the public and by charity bookshops. Check out their facebook page:
www.facebook.com/wordonthewater

The Royal Institution
FREE Monthly Book club London
The **Free** monthly book club dedicated to great fiction books with a science theme. If you're an interested reader who has something to say, then go along.
www.rigb.org

Riverside Walk Market
Southbank London SE1
This weekly market specialises in new and second-hand books and prints. Situated underneath Waterloo bridge on the South side of the Thames Sat-Sun.

Museums

Museum Lates
After-hours museum visits are the perfect cultural night out and Londoners have embraced the concept with enthusiasm. What's not to like about checking out a new exhibition whilst socialising, often with music. Many Museums take part in the after hours visits check out the website of the Museum of your choice to see if they participate.

Aircraft Museums

* British Airways Heritage Centre London
The British Airways Heritage collection has existed since the formation of British Airways. The collection comprises of an extensive document archive recording the formation development and operations of British Airways and its predecessor companies as well as memorabilia and artefacts.
Visits need to be booked see website:
Admission FREE
www.britishairways.com/travel/museum-collection

Interesting Fact
British Airways
Heritage Centre
With over 130 uniforms from the 1930s to the present day, as well as a large collection of aircraft models and pictures.

Royal Air Force Museum London NW9
The Royal Air Force Museum in London is Britain's only national Museum dedicated wholly to aviation. The Museum offers a unique experience to the visitor and the exhibits complement each other. The Museum tells the story of aviation from early bi-planes to the latest jets.
Admission FREE
www.rafmuseum.org.uk

Architecture Museums

New London Architecture Museum
NLA is an independent forum for debate about the future shape of the city and a permanent information resource about what's happening in architecture, planning, development and construction across the capital.
Admission FREE
www.newlondonarchitecture.org

Interesting Fact
New London Architecture
There is a permanent exhibition/display of the plans of the Olympic Park.

Thrifty Tip
NLA FREE Events
New London Architecture also has many FREE
events exhibitions and talks throughout the year
see website:
www.newlondonarchitecture.org

Soane Museum London WC2
The architect John Soane designed this house to
live in, but also as a setting for his antiquities
and his works of art. The collections include
over 250 historical architectural models
including examples of furniture and decorative
art. There are also paintings by Hogarth and
Caneletto.
Admission FREE
www.soane.org

Interesting Fact
Sir John Soane
John Soane was an architect who specialised in
Neo Classical style, his work includes the
original Bank of England Building, and The
Dulwich Picture Gallery.

Thrifty Tip
Soane Museum Candlelight Tours
The Museum is lit by candlelight on the first
Tuesday of each month, between 6 and 9pm.
This event is extremely popular so they limit the
number of people allowed in to the Museum
during the course of the evening. They issue
tickets from 5:30pm to the first 200 people in
the queue.
Admission FREE
www.soane.org

Archaeology Museums

All Hallows by the Tower London EC3
The under croft museum is in part of the original Saxon church and contains a collection of Roman and Saxon artefacts including Roman mosaics and pottery
Admission FREE
www.allhallowsbythetower.org.uk

Thrifty Tip
All Hallows by the Tower
FREE Organ Concerts
Regular organ concerts take place at All Hallows at lunchtime on Thursdays.
All concerts start at 1.10pm and finish by 2pm unless otherwise indicated.

Petrie Museum UCL London WC1
The Petrie Museum houses an estimated 80,000 objects, making it one of the greatest collections of Egyptian and Sudanese archaeology in the world. It illustrates life in the Nile Valley from prehistory through the time of the pharaohs, the Ptolemaic, Roman and Coptic periods to the Islamic period.
Admission FREE
www.ucl.ac.uk/museums/petrie

Institute of Archaeology
London WC1
The Institute of Archaeology houses fine teaching and reference collections. They include prehistoric ceramics and stone artifacts from many parts of the world as well as collections of Classical Greek and Roman ceramics.

There are also extensive collections of archaeobotanical and zoo archaeological material which act as a primary source for the identification of plant and animal remains.
www.ucl.ac.uk/museums/archaeology

Art Design & Fashion Museums

2 Willow Road Hampstead NW3

This unique Modernist home was designed by architect Ernö Goldfinger in 1939 for himself and his family. With surprising design details that were ground-breaking at the time and yet still feel fresh today. The house also contains the Goldfingers' impressive collection of modern art, intriguing personal possessions and innovative furniture.

Admission Concessions £3 Adults £6
www.nationaltrust.org.uk/2-willow-road

Interesting Fact
Ernö Goldfinger

Ian Fleming named James Bond's adversary and villain Auric Goldfinger after Ernő.

7 Hammersmith Terrace London

No 7 Hammersmith Terrace is a tall terraced house on the River Thames at Hammersmith in west London. Its Georgian exterior hides a secret the decoration and furnishings preserved as they were in the lifetime of its owner the printer Emery Walker (1851-1933). The house is the last authentic Arts and Crafts interior in Britain.

Admission by guided tours only see website for prices and details:
www.emerywalker.org.uk

Interesting Fact
Emery Walker & William Morris
Emery Walker was a great friend and mentor to William Morris.
www.emerywalker.org.uk

575 Wandsworth Road London
Over the last twenty years of his life, Khadambi Asalache (a Kenyan-born poet, novelist, philosopher of mathematics and British civil servant) decorated the interior of his modest terraced 19th century house in south west London with his own crafted fretwork and decorative painting. He also displayed textiles and everyday objects from East Africa.
Admission by tour only see website for full details:
www.575wandsworthroadnt.wordpress.com /the-house

Crystal Palace Museum London SE19
The Crystal Palace was an iron and plate glass building created by Joseph Paxton to house the Exhibition of the Industry of Nations that was to be staged in Hyde Park London in 1851. The Palace was tragically destroyed in a spectacular fire in November 1936, and the Museum is dedicated to keeping alive its memory with photographs and displays of original documents and ceramics.
Admission FREE
www.crystalpalacemuseum.org.uk

Interesting Fact
Crystal Palace
The Crystal Palace was also famous for its magnificent water towers that were designed by Isambard Kingdom Brunel.
www.crystalpalacemuseum.org.uk/museum.html

Design Museum London SE1
The Design Museum Collection is made up by over 2000 objects that range from the early Modernism of the 1900s to the cutting edge of contemporary design. The Collection includes furniture, lighting, domestic appliances and communications technology.
Students & Concessions £7
Admission under 12's FREE
Admission to the Shop and Café is FREE
www.designmuseum.org

Fashion and Textile Museum London SE1
The Fashion and Textile Museum is a cutting edge centre for contemporary fashion, textiles and jewellery.
Admission £5.50 for Students and Concessions
Under 12s FREE
www.ftmlondon.org

Interesting Fact
Fashion and Textile Museum
The museum was founded by iconic British designer Zandra Rhodes.
www.ftmlondon.org

Garden Museum London SE1

The Museum was set up in 1977 in order to rescue from demolition the abandoned ancient church of St Mary's which is the burial place of John Tradescant the first great gardener and plant-hunter in British history.

His tomb is the centrepiece of a knot garden planted with the flowers which grew in his London garden four centuries ago.
Admission Students £3 Senior Citizens £4 Adults £5
Admission FREE (for under 16s those on Jobseekers and carers of disabled people).
www.gardenmuseum.org.uk

* Thrifty Tip
Garden Museum
Seasonal Saturdays

The museum also hosts seasonal Saturdays these are drop in sessions for children, parents and carers where they can make/or plant something together to take home - Suitable for children aged 2 - 10.
Admission FREE to the Museum for families taking part in the activities.
www.gardenmuseum.org.uk

Thrifty Tip
Garden Museum
FREE Guided Tours

FREE guided tours on the last Tuesday of every month.
www.gardenmuseum.org.uk
Geffrey Museum Shoreditch London E2

The Geoffrey Museum is one of London's best-loved museums. It is devoted to the history of

the home, showing how homes and gardens reflect changes in society, style and taste over the past 400 years. Focusing on the urban living rooms and gardens of the English middle classes A must visit for anyone with a love of period homes and gardens.
Admission FREE
www.geffrye-museum.org.uk

Interesting Fact
Sir Robert Geoffrey
The Geoffrey Museum is set in the former almshouses of the Ironmongers' company, built in 1714 with a bequest from Sir Robert Geoffrey and sold to London County Council in 1911.

* Thrifty Tip
Geoffrey Museum
FREE Activities
FREE Holiday activities for children.

Kelmscott House London W6
Kelmscott House dates from the 1780s and is now chiefly associated with the designer, poet and socialist William Morris who lived here from 1878 until his death. The Society has a comprehensive collection of Morris and Company wallpapers, watercolour designs, and a selection of textiles, ranging from rugs and woven hangings to printed cottons, silks and embroideries.
Visits by guided tour only – donation
See website for details:
www.williammorrissociety.org

Kinetica Museum London E8
The Museum provides an international platform
for contemporary artists working in the realm of
interdisciplinary new media art.
The museum does not have gallery space so you
can not visit however there are many
**FREE Exhibitions throughout the year see
website for listing.**
www.kinetica-museum.org

Leighton House Museum London W14
The former home and studio workspace of the
Victorian artist Frederic Leighton. The
centerpiece of the house is the famous Arab
Hall. Lined with hundreds of sixteenth and
seventeenth century tiles from Damascus, and
inlaid with Egyptian woodwork, the hall is a
striking celebration of the Middle East in
London.
Admission Concessions £3 Adults £5
www.rbkc.gov.uk

Interesting Fact
Frederic Leighton
Frederic Leighton (1830-1896), was one of the
most famous British artists of the Victorian age,
establishing an international standing and
reputation.

Martinware Pottery Collection
Southall Library London UB2
Wallace, Walter, Edwin and Charles Martin,
were pioneers in the production of studio
pottery, some beautifully formed and expertly
decorated.

They are noted for their famous bird jars. A small collection of Martinware is still available to view by appointment at Southall Library. Please telephone to book appointment to view
Tel: **0208 825 7259**
Admission FREE

Interesting Fact
Martinware Pottery
Wallace Martin and Brothers started producing pottery in Fulham in 1873. In 1877, the brothers moved to a disused soap works on the canal in Southall.

Museum of Brands London W11
It's all there the brands and packs, posters and adverts, fads and fashions, toys and games. Evocative and inspiring, it's a kaleidoscope of images and iconic brands. A very nostalgic place to visit, it brings back memories of bygone era. Admission Concessions £4.00 Adults £6.50 Children £2.25
www.museumofbrands.com/index.html

Museum of Domestic Design
& Architecture
London NW9
The collections include wallpapers, textiles, designs, books, catalogues and magazines from the late nineteenth to the late twentieth century. They are a great resource if you are interested in the history of domestic interiors, or if you are looking for visual inspiration for creative projects.

Many touring exhibitions view online or call to book visit.
Admission FREE
www.moda.mdx.ac.uk

UCL Art Museum London WC1
Over 10,000 works of art make up the collections at UCL from the 1500s to the present day. Works separated by centuries are linked by a desire to experiment with new materials, theories, and reproduction techniques in order to produce new meanings, share ideas and inspire.
Admission FREE
www.ucl.ac.uk/museums

Victoria and Albert Museum London SW7
The world's greatest museum of art and design, with ceramics, glass, textiles, costumes, silver, ironwork, jewellery, furniture, medieval objects, sculpture, prints and printmaking, drawings and photographs, these are among the largest important and most comprehensive in the world.
Admission FREE
www.vam.ac.uk

Interesting Fact
Victoria & Albert Museum John Madjeski Garden Fountains
London SW7
The V&A's beautiful courtyard is home to a beautiful lake fringed with water jets.

Steps lead into the Fountain so that it can function as a paddling pool in hot weather.

Thrifty Tip
Victoria & Albert Museum
British Galleries Tour join this daily one hour tour which introduces the V&A's stunning British Galleries which house the most comprehensive collection of British Art and Design on view anywhere in the world.

William Morris Gallery Walthamstow
Discover the life and works of Britain's most inspiring designer at the newly-refurbished William Morris Gallery in Walthamstow, London. Explore the internationally-renowned collections of the William Morris Gallery and learn more about the life and work of this remarkable individual and his artistic collaborators.
Admission FREE
www.wmgallery.org.uk

Interesting Fact
The Crafts Council
The Crafts Council's goal is to make the UK the best place to make, see, collect and learn about contemporary craft. They are committed to providing opportunities for the public to engage with contemporary craft through the national Crafts Council Collection. They have an exhibitions programme of events and exhibitions many
of which are **FREE** see website.
www.craftscouncil.org.uk

Ballet Museums

London Jewish Cultural Centre
Pavlova Memorial (Ivy House)
London NW1

Ivy House was the home and studio of legendary ballerina Anna Pavlova. It was in this room that she did class, rehearsed and taught with many of the stars of the day.
Visits by Appointment only
Tel: 0208 457 5000
www.westhampsteadschoolofdance.co.uk

* Whitelodge Museum & Ballet Resources
Centre Richmond

White Lodge Museum and Ballet Resource Centre is the first dedicated ballet museum in the UK. It is housed within White Lodge - a Grade I listed building, which is now the home of The Royal Ballet Lower School. Visitors to White Lodge Museum can learn about the daily life of students at The Royal Ballet School, the history and development of Classical ballet and the fascinating story of White Lodge itself.
Visits must be booked see website
Admission FREE
www.royal-ballet-school.org.uk

Interesting Facts
White Lodge Museum

Displays feature material from the Royal Ballet School Collections, including Margot Fonteyn's ballet shoe, the death mask of Anna Pavlova and the school reports of famous alumni.

The Ballet School at White Lodge has a Replica of the Royal Opera House stage.

Interesting Fact
Royal Ballet School
Famous Alumni of the Royal Ballet School include Dame Margot Fonteyn, Sir Kenneth MacMillan, Dame Antoinette Sibley, Sir Anthony Dowell, Anya Linden, Jonathan Cope and Darcey Bussell.
www.royal-ballet-school.org.uk

Cartoons & Animation Museums

* Cartoon Museum London WC1
The Cartoon Museum exhibits the very finest examples of British cartoons caricature and comic art from the 18th century to the present day.
Admission Concession £4 Students £3 Adults £5.50
Under 18s FREE
www.cartoonmuseum.org

* Thrifty Tip
Cartoon Museum
FREE Cartooning activities for families 2nd Saturday of every month see website:
www.cartoonmuseum.org

Childhood & Toy Museums

* Museum of Childhood (V&A)
London E2
The V&A Museum of Childhood houses the
Museum's collection of childhood-related
objects and artifacts, spanning the 1600s to the
present day. As well as toys, dolls, dolls'
houses, games and puzzles, the Museum also
has a wealth of objects relating to many other
aspects of childhood.
Admission FREE
www.museumofchildhood.org.uk

* Thrifty Tip
Museum of Childhood
FREE Activities
Storytelling, arts & crafts, treasure hunts,
workshops, tours and daily activities.
See website:
www.museumofchildhood.org.uk

* Pollock's Toy Museum
Fitzrovia London W1
Nearly every kind of toy imaginable turns up
here from all over the world and from different
time periods. It's a fascinating exhibition of toy
theatres, teddy bears, dolls, doll's houses, board
games, folk toys, nursery furniture, and
mechanical toys.
Children £3 Concessions £5 Adults £6
www.pollockstoymuseum.com

Cinema & Film Museums

* Cinema Museum London SE11

London's Cinema Museum is devoted to keeping alive the spirit of cinema going from the days before the multiplex. The Museum houses a unique collection of artefacts memorabilia and equipment that preserves the history of cinema going from the 1890s to the present day. At the moment it is only possible to view the Museum collection with a guided tour

Tour Prices £7 for Concessions and Children
www.cinemamuseum.org.uk

Interesting Fact
Cinema Museum
The Cinema museum was once a workhouse; ironically it is here that Charlie Chaplin was first processed into the workhouse as a nine year old.

* London Film Museum Covent Garden London WC2

The London Film Museum is the only film museum of its kind in Great Britain, supporting the Film Industry and the talent within it. This creative hotspot boasts dynamic exhibition layouts that will wow any visitors especially film buffs.
Admission FREE
www.londonfilmmuseum.com

* London Film Museum
City Hall Southbank
London Film Museum has original pieces which
include original costumes (Batman, Superman
Star Wars to name but a few) and props from
British films, including the Rank Organisation
Gong used in their opening titles. However
visiting LFM at City Hall is not Free see website
for pricing.
www.londonfilmmuseum.com

Thrifty Tips for Film Lovers

BP Outdoor Film Screenings During
June/July Venues Include:
At the outdoor screenings you can enjoy world
class opera and ballet in true alfresco style.
Venues include The Scoop, and Trafalgar
Square.
Annual event for listings see website:
www.roh.org.uk/about/bp-big-screens

British Library London NW1
The Future Shorts Festival is the biggest pop up
film festival of its kind, showcasing the most
exciting short films from around the world. For
listings see website:
www.bl.uk

Goeth Institute London SW7
FREE Events throughout the year including
film screenings
www.goethe.de/ins/gb/lon

* Museum of London Docklands
Regular FREE activities for families, and FREE
film screenings see website.
www.museumoflondon.org.uk/docklands

National Portrait Gallery London WC2
Late Shift - enjoy a wide range of events
including film screenings
Admission FREE
www.npg.org.uk

Somerset House Film Screenings
Each summer, The Edmond J. Safra Fountain
Court hosts London's most beautiful open-air
cinema; Film4 Summer Screen. A highlight of
the city's summer calendar, the series features a
range of films, all showing on a state-of-the-art
screen with full surround sound. For prices and
details see website:
www.somersethouse.org.uk/film

The Roxy Bar & Screen London SE1
Screenings take place in the back area of
Roxy Sun – Weds, for full details see website:
Admission FREE (unless otherwise stated)
www.roxybarandscreen.com

* FREE Film Making Workshops

FREE Film Making Workshops
London SE15
The film making workshops are part of the Free
Film Making Festivals.

If you would like to take part and improve your filmmaking skills check out the website:
www.freefilmfestivals.org

Crime & Punishment Museums

Clink Museum London SE1
The Clink Prison Museum is built upon the original site of the Clink Prison. The Prison dates back to 1144 making it one of England's oldest, Prisons. Visitors can handle original artefacts, and also have the opportunity to view and hear some amazing stories. Admission Concessions £5.50
www.clink.co.uk

River Thames Police Museum London E1
The Thames River Police Museum offers visitors a unique insight into the history of the World's first police force. Exhibits include uniforms and documents, which trace the history of the Thames River Police. There is also a fine collection of the every day "Hardware" of policing from handcuffs to cutlasses.
See website for details of how to arrange a visit.
www.thamespolicemuseum.org.uk

Interesting Fact
UK Police Force
One time Prime Minister of UK Sir Robert Peel helped to create the modern concept of the Police Force whilst working as Home Secretary he drafted the Metropolitan Police Bill in 1829.

To this day Police offers are known as Bobbies (Bobbie being a nickname for Robert).

Cultural Museums

* British Museum
London WC1
The Museum is dedicated to human history and culture. Its permanent collection, numbers some eight million works. With a vast collection of world art and artefacts it is widely considered to be one of the world's greatest museums of human history and culture. Astronomy and scientific development is also covered.
The Tree of Life in the African Gallery is a highlight.
Admission FREE
www.britishmuseum.org

Interesting Fact
British Museum
Reading Room
Many great writers and researchers have done their work at the British Museum reading room. These include Karl Marx, Lenin, Bram Stoker and Sir Arthur Conan Doyle.

* Thrifty Tip
British Museum
FREE Activities
Free trails, workshops and activities for family visits see website:
www.britishmuseum.org

Thrifty Tip
British Museum
FREE Gallery Talks and Tours available daily:

Black Cultural Archives Museum
London SW9
Black Cultural Archives was founded in 1981
to collect, preserve and celebrate the
contributions Black people have made to the
culture, society and heritage of the UK. The
growing archive collection offers insight into
the history of people of African descent in
Britain.
Open on Wednesdays by appointment only
Admission FREE
www.bcaheritage.org.uk

Jewish Museum
London NW1
The Museum expanded to reflect the diverse
roots and social history of Jewish people across
London, including the experiences of refugees
from Nazism. It also developed an acclaimed
programme of Holocaust and anti-racist
education.
Admission Concessions £6.50 and Child (5-16)
£3.50
Admission Only £3.50 to visit the Jewish
Museum on Thursday Evenings
www.jewishmuseum.org.uk

Interesting Fact
Jewish Museum
Amy Winehouse Exhibition

The Jewish Museum is staging an original exhibition about Amy Winehouse, co-curated with her brother Alex and sister-in-law Riva. It is an intimate and moving exhibition about a much loved sister.
May-September 2013.

Elite Schools Museums

Eton School Museum of Eton Life Berks
The Museum of Eton Life tells the story of the foundation of the College in 1440 and provides a glimpse into the world of the Eton schoolboy past and present. The Museum contains over 400 exhibits, find out about work, games punishment, and some of the customs of the past.
Admission FREE
www.etoncollege.com

Interesting Fact
Old Etonians
There are many well-known old Etonians including HRH Prince William, HRH Prince Harry, Charles Spencer, David Cameron (UK Prime Minister) George Orwell (Novelist), and James Bond creator Ian Flemming (Novelist).
www.etoncollege.com

Harrow School
Old Speech Room Gallery & Museum
The Old Speech Room was converted into a gallery by Alan Irvine in 1976 as a repository for the School's distinguished collection of antiquities and fine art.

The collections comprise Egyptian, Greek and
Etruscan antiquities, modern British paintings,
Japanese prints, photographs, sculpture,
manuscripts, rare Bibles, and more.
See website for opening times.
Admission FREE
www.harrowschool.org.uk

Interesting Fact
Harrow School
Old Harrovians include Royalty, Politicians and
Prime Ministers. Byron, Sheridan and Sir
Winston Churchill were pupils. Churchill's
painting *A Distant View of Venice,* 1929 is
one of the highlights of the Gallery collection.

Thrifty Tip
Harrow School
During term-time, Harrow School musicians
entertain with the Lunchtime Concert series
every Tuesday in St Mary's Church, Harrow on
the Hill.

Westminster School
London SW1
The Royal College of St. Peter in Westminster,
better known as Westminster School, is one of
Britain's leading independent schools, with the
highest Oxford & Cambridge acceptance rate of
any secondary school or college in Britain.
www.Westminster.org.uk

Interesting Fact
Westminster School

188

Alumni include Sir Christopher Wren, Lord Andrew Lloyd-Webber, Helena Bonham-Carter, Tony Benn, Nigel Lawson, and Nick Clegg MP.

Interesting Fact
TS Elliott
TS Eliot was a teacher at Highgate Private School London in 1915 and taught the young John Betjeman.

Museums Fire

* Fire Brigade Museum London SE1
Explore the museum's fire station, once part of the original Southwark fire station in the 1870s and home to a unique collection of historical fire engines.

Travel through time and discover why the Great Fire of London was so influential to the history of firefighting.
Concessions children and groups £3 per person.
www.london-fire.gov.uk/OurMuseum.asp

Interesting Fact
Great Fire of London
The Great Fire of London swept through the city in September1666, remarkably the death toll was only six people.

Geology Museums

* Geology Collections

UCL London WC1

The Rock Room is one of UCL's registered museums and has a history stretching back to around 1855. The collection includes not only rocks, minerals and fossils collected over the last 175 years, but also some of historical importance.

The highlights include the Johnston-Lavis Volcano logical collection, the Planetary Science Collection and the Micropalaeontological collections. The Rock Room is open every Friday between 13:00 - 15:00.

Admission FREE

www.ucl.ac.uk/museums/geology

* Geology Museum
(Natural History Museum)
London SW7

Find out about Fossils, minerals and rocks and learn how to identify them.

Discover how Diamonds are formed and how they can be used in science. Also find out about the mineral that matches Kryptonite.

Admission FREE

www.nhm.ac.uk

* Interesting Fact
Geology Museum at Natural History Museum

Museum Highlights include the Earthquake room with earthquake simulator (Reopening October 2013).

Royal Geographic Society
London SW7
Memorabilia including many maps from some
of the world's great explorers including
Livingstone and Shackleton available to view.
The Society also put on exhibitions.
Admission FREE
www.rgs.org

Interesting Facts
David Livingstone
Livingstones meeting with Stanley in November
1871 gave rise to the popular quotation "Dr.
Livingstone, I presume?"

David Livingstone's resting place is
Westminster Abbey London.

Food & Drink Museums

Twining's Museum
London
A small museum where you can see some
fascinating stuff including old teapots and
caddies and some lovely old pictures of the
Twining family.

Thrifty Tip
Twining's
FREE Tea Tasting available
http://shop.twinings.co.uk/shop/Strand

History & Industrial Museums

Brent Museum (Grange Museum)
Neasden London NW10
The Brent Museum of Community History
holds hundreds of objects relating to the history
of Brent since around 1800 including the
Olympic torch from the 1948 Olympic Games
and signed football from when England won
the World Cup in 1966.
www.brent.gov.uk/museum

Eton College
Natural History Museum Eton
The museum was opened in 1875 to house the
Thackeray Collection of British Birds and other
collections. It now houses over 15,000
specimens, donated from the nineteenth century
onwards.
The Museum is used extensively for teaching
biology and geology as well as being open to the
public and visited by numerous schools and
outside groups.
www.etoncollege.com

Greenwich Heritage Centre & Museum
London SE18
At Greenwich Heritage Centre you can learn
about the fascinating history of London
Borough of Greenwich from earlier times to the
present day.
Admission FREE
www.greenwichheritage.org

* Thrifty Tip
Greenwich
As well as its amazing Museums and Park
Greenwich has a great market (where you can
find Antiques, Crafts and original Artwork),
shops and cafes. There are also regular FREE
events taking place in Greenwich see website
for full details:
www.visitgreenwich.org.uk

Island History Trust London E14
A community history project dedicated to
recording and preserving the history of the Isle
of Dogs and the people who live there.
Visits by appointment only
www.islandhistory.org.uk

* Islington Museum London EC1
Islington Museum opened in May 2008 in a
brand new space under Finsbury Library. Learn
about Lenin's time in Islington, May
Woollstonecraft (best known for *A*
Vindication of the Rights of Women- she
argues that women are not inferior to men).
**www.islington.gov.uk/islington/history-
heritage**

Interesting Fact
Astoria/Rainbow Theatre
Islington London N4
At the Islington Museum you can find details of
the amazing Astoria Finsbury Park. In its hay
day it was one of the greatest Music Venues in
London.

The Beach Boys (their Album *Live in London* was recorded here), The Beetles, Jimi Hendrix (It is here where Hendrix first burnt a guitar), The Jackson's, Queen, The Walker Brothers, The Who and many more played at this famous London venue throughout the 60s and 70s.

* Thrifty Tip
Islington Museum
Arsenal Football Club Exhibition
Islington Museum will be holding an Arsenal Football Club Centenary Exhibition in conjunction with the club from September 2013.

* Lavender Pond Pump House
Rotherhithe London SE16
Lavender Pond Pump house is an interesting piece of architectural history that sits beside the River Thames. It is open to the public throughout the week and has a small museum attached. The area is rich in industrial history.
Admission FREE
www.southwark.gov.uk

* Museum of London
London EC2
Experience an unforgettable journey through the capital's turbulent past to the present day, including Roman Gallery/London Wall, and Great Fire of London display.

A highlight is the opportunity to see the Mayor's golden coach.

Other highlights include an Art Deco Lift that was once a part of Selfridge's store.
Admission FREE
www.museumoflondon.org.uk

* Interesting Fact
Museum of London
The Museum also houses some of the costumes used in the opening and closing ceremonies of the London Games 2012.

* Thrifty Tip
Museum of London
FREE Activities loads of fun things to do for kids of all ages see website for details:
www.museumoflondon.org.uk

* Museum of London Docklands
Discover London's long history as a port through stories of trade, migration and commerce. Highlights include The Sailor town gallery a full size reconstruction of the dark, winding streets of Victorian Wapping. The gallery attempts to recreate the contemporary description of the area as "both foul and picturesque". The area was a maze of streets, lanes and alleys.
Admission FREE
www.museumoflondon.org.uk/docklands

* Thrifty Tip
FREE Activities
Museum of London Docklands
Regular FREE activities for families and FREE film screenings see website.
www.museumoflondon.org.uk/docklands

National Archives Museum Kew
The National Archives is the official archive and it contains over 1000 years of UK history it also has the public records office. There is also a museum, which displays key documents such as the Doomsday Book and has exhibitions on various topics using material from its collections.
Admission FREE
www.nationalarchives.gov.uk

Interesting Fact
National Archives
Important documents held include Shakespeare's will, and the trial record of Charles 1.

* Thrifty Tip
National Archives FREE Talks
They hold a range FREE public talks on records of interest, to training courses for archivists and academics.

* Natural History Museum
London SW7
The museum is home to life and earth science specimens comprising some 70 million items within five main collections: Botany, Entomology, Mineralogy, Paleontology and Zoology. Many of the collections have great historical and scientific value, such as specimens collected by Darwin.
Admission FREE
www.nhm.ac.uk

* Natural History Museum

Highlights include a life size model of a Blue Whale and Blue Whale skeletons, the Dinosaurs room where you can learn all about the prehistoric creatures and the new interactive Attenborough Studios.

*Natural History Museum
Sensational Butterflies

During the Spring/Summer the Museum's front lawn is alive with the popular outdoor butterfly exhibition, with chomping caterpillars and beautiful butterflies this is a must for all Butterfly lovers.

Literature & Poetry Museums

The Browning Room
Marylebone Church London NW1

Robert Browning and Elizabeth Barrett Married at this church in 1846 (Their marriage certificate is preserved in the church archives). There is a Commemorative window dedicated to Browning and Barrett and busts of the pair.
www.stmarylebone.org

Interesting Fact
Marylebone Church
Healing Prayer

There are services of Prayer for Healing offered at this church see website for full details. Also an informal healing prayer group meets at 2.30 - 4 pm on the 1st Friday afternoon each month.

Interesting Fact
Elizabeth Barrett Browning
The sonnet, "*How Do I Love Thee,*" was written by Elizabeth Barrett Browning for Robert Browning.

Carlyle's House Chelsea London SW3
Preserved since 1895 this writer's house in the heart of one of London's most famous creative quarters tells the story of Thomas and Jane Carlyle. The couple a much-loved celebrity couple of the 19th-century literary world. Learn about Carlyle's influence on William Morris and the Pre-Raphaelites.
Admission Concessions £2.60 Adult £5.10
www.nationaltrust.org.uk/carlyles-house

Interesting Fact
Jane Carlyle
Jane Carlyle is considered one of the best women letter writers in the English language. You can read Thomas and Jane's letters online at The Carlyle's Letters Online website.
www.nationaltrust.org.uk/carlyles-house

* Dickens House
London WC1
Charles Dickens's lived here from 1837 until 1839. He described it as 'my house in town'. The Museum was opened in 1925 and has become the world's finest Dickens-related collection.
Admission Concession £6
www.dickensmuseum.com

Interesting Fact
Dickens House
Oliver Twist and *Nicholas Nickleby* were both written at the house.

* Thrifty Tip
Dickens House
FREE Events
FREE Events organised throughout the year see website for full details:
www.dickensmuseum.com

Dr Johnson House London EC4
Dr Johnson's House is a small historic town house in the City of London. It was in the top floor garret that Dr Johnson compiled the English Dictionary. The house has a dedicated team of volunteers who together run a vibrant programmer of education, exhibitions and events.
Admission Concessions £3.50 Child £1.50
www.drjohnsonshouse.org

Interesting Fact
Dr Johnson
Dr Samuel Johnson was born in 1709 in Lichfield, Staffordshire. He rose to become one of the greatest literary figures of the eighteenth century, most famously compiling *A Dictionary of the English Language.*

* Thrifty Tip
Dr Johnson House
FREE Events

Many FREE Events throughout the year see
website for details
www.drjohnsonshouse.org

Dr Johnson's
Famous Quote about London
"Why, Sir, you find no man, at all intellectual,
who is willing to leave London. No, Sir, when a
man is tired of London, he is tired of life; for
there is in London all that life can afford."

Keats House
London NW3
The romantic poet John Keats lived here from
1818 to 1820. The setting inspired some of his
most memorable poetry. The collection is
comprised of a variety of Keats related material
including books, paintings, letters written by
Keats, and the engagement ring given by Keats
to his fiancée, Fanny Brawne.
Admission FREE for Under 17s
Concessions £3.00 Adults £5.00
www.cityoflondon.gov.uk

Interesting Fact
John Keats
Keats became one of the principal poets of the
English Romantic movement along with Lord
Byron and Percy Bysshe Shelley.
www.cityoflondon.gov.uk

Medical Museums

The Anaesthesia Heritage Centre
London W1

The Anaesthesia Heritage Centre collection encompasses the entire history of anaesthesia, from Morton's demonstration of ether inhalation in 1846 to modern anaesthetic machines and appliances still in use today. An archive and library provide excellent facilities for research. Visitors need to book.
Admission FREE
www.medicalmuseums.org/Anaesthesia-Heritage-Centre

British Optical Museum
London WC2

Founded by J. H. Sutcliffe of the British Optical Association in 1901, this is a remarkable museum collection with over eighteen thousand objects. This includes over 3000 pairs of spectacles, and designer eyewear of the twenty-first, century as well as historic examples of other optical devices.
visit the museum (by prior appointment)
Admission FREE
www.college-optometrists.org

Interesting Fact
British Optical Museum

The Museum possesses the spectacles of various famous personalities including Dr Johnson, C.P. Snow, Ronnie Corbett as well as a pair made for Johnny Depp (which he rejected).

Interesting Fact
Bifocal Spectacles
Invented by Benjamin Franklin
In 1784 Ben Franklin developed bifocal glasses.
He was getting old and was having trouble
seeing both up-close and at a distance. Getting
tired of switching between two types of glasses,
he devised a way to have both types of lenses fit
into the frame.

British Red Cross Museum
London EC2
The British Red Cross museum and
archives contain a fascinating portrait of their
humanitarian work, from their beginnings in
1870 to their contribution in today's society.
The museum and archive collection is
available for research purposes by prior
appointment.
www.redcross.org.uk/About-us/Who-we-are/Museum-and-archives

Dental Museum London W1
The Dental Museum is the place to find out
about the history of dental care in the UK. With
over 20,000 items the museum has the largest
collection of material relating to the history of
dentistry in the UK.
Admission FREE
www.bda.org/museum/about-the-museum

Interesting Fact
Lillian Lindsay Dentist
Lilian Lindsay was the first female to qualify as a
dentist in the UK, and she became the first
female president of the British Dental
Association.

Fleming Museum
St Mary's Hospital London W2
St Mary's Hospital is home to the Alexander
Fleming Laboratory Museum. Visitors to the
Museum can see Fleming's laboratory,
and explore the story of Fleming and the
discovery and development of penicillin
through displays and video.
Admission Concessions £2.00 Adults: £4.00
www.imperial.nhs.uk/aboutus/museumsan
darchives

Interesting Facts
Alexander Fleming
Alexander Fleming discovered the antibiotic
penicillin at St Mary's Hospital in 1928; it earned
him a Nobel Prize.

Alexander Flemmings is buried at St Paul's
Cathedral

* Florence Nightingale Museum
St Thomas's Hospital
London SE1
Florence Nightingale became a living legend as
the 'Lady with the Lamp'. She led the nurses
caring for thousands of soldiers during the
Crimean War.
The Museums three pavilions tell the real story
of Florence Nightingale, the world of the
Victorians and her impact on nursing today.
Admission Concession £4.80 Adults £5.80
www.florence-nightingale.co.uk

Interesting Fact
Florence Nightingale
The Nursing school at St Thomas's Hospital is called The Florence Nightingale School of Nursing and Midwifery; Nurses who train there are called "Nightingales".

Foundling Museum
Brunswick Square London WC1N
The Foundling Museum houses significant collections of eighteenth-century art, interiors, social history and music.
Admission Concessions £5
Admission FREE for children up to 16 years
www.foundlingmuseum.org.uk

Interesting Facts
Foundling Museum
Fate, Hope & Charity brings to light the untold stories of the Foundling Hospital tokens, small everyday objects left by mothers with their babies at the Hospital between1741-1760.

William Hogarth (1697-1764) devoted over twenty-five years of his life to the Foundling Hospital, becoming the leading artistic contributor to the Foundling Hospital Art Collection.

Great Ormond Street Hospital Museum
London WC1
The Museum of Great Ormond Street Hospital (GOSH) is devoted to the history of the hospital and personalities connected with the hospital since its inception in 1852.

The museum shows artefacts, artworks, photographs and documents. There is also a collection of rare & multi-national 'Peter Pan' editions.
Admission FREE
www.medicalmuseums.org/Great-Ormond-Street-Hospital-Museum

Interesting Fact
Great Ormond Street Hospital
JM Barrie (Author) gave all the rights to his book Peter Pan to Great Ormond Street Hospital in 1929, and this was later confirmed when he died in 1937. There is a bronze statue of "Peter Pan" at the hospital.

Hunterian Museum
Royal College of Surgeons London WC2
Exhibits include the skeleton body coat - find out about the different size and shape of the bones in your body. You can wear the organ tabbard to see if you can work out how your heart, lungs, stomach, kidneys and other major organs fit together inside of you. The museum also contains preserved human and animal remains showing normal anatomy as well as diseases.
Admission FREE
www.rcseng.ac.uk

Thrifty Tip
Hunterian Museum
FREE Talks
FREE talks cover a wide range of subjects relating to the museum collections and the history of surgery.

Royal London Hospital Museum
London E1

The Museum is located in the former crypt of the former hospital Church. The Museum has revamped sections on the history of the hospital since its foundation in 1740, Joseph Merrick (the 'Elephant Man') and former London Hospital nurses Edith Cavell and Eva Luckes.
www.bartsandthelondon.nhs.uk

Interesting Fact
Joseph Merrick

Joseph Merrick (1862 - 1890), was an English man with severe deformities who was also cruelly named the Elephant Man. He became well known in London after surgeon Frederick Treves rescued him (he was being used as a circus act) and invited him to live at the London Hospital.

Interesting Fact
Edith Cavell

Edith Cavel 1865-1915 was a British Nurse who trained at the Royal London Hospital. Nurse Cavel was celebrated for saving the lives of soldiers from all sides during World War 1.

For this she was arrested, court marshaled found guilty and sentenced to death by German Firing Squad.

Old Operating Theatre Museum
London SE1
The Old Operating Theatre Museum is one of the most unusual museums in London. The Operating Theatre is the oldest in Europe and found in a unique space in the Herb Garret of St Thomas Church. The Theatre itself is a shocking reminder of the harsh reality of life before modern science and technology.
Admission Concessions £3.50 Adult £5
www.thegarret.org.uk/opening.htm

Old Operating Theatre Museum
Herb Garratt London SE1
When St Thomas's Church was rebuilt in 1703 it had an unusually large Garret in the roof space. This was used by the St Thomas's Apothecary to store and cure herbs.
Admission Concessions £5 Adults £6.20
www.thegarret.org.uk/opening.htm

Royal Hospital Chelsea London SW3
Royal Hospital Chelsea is home to "The Men in Scarlet', the Chelsea Pensioners. The Museum is mostly composed of artefacts left by deceased In-Pensioners. The entrance Hall is dedicated to the memory of the Duke of Wellington, and a variety of objects associated with him.
Admission FREE
www.chelsea-pensioners.co.uk/home

Interesting Fact
Royal Hospital Chelsea
Sir Christopher Wren built the original Royal
Hospital Chelsea building which is a real
architectural gem.

Thrifty Tip
Royal Hospital Chelsea
Easter & Christmas Services are helped in the
chapel all welcome.

Royal College of Physicians Museum
London
The Royal College of Physicians is the oldest
medical college in England. Since its foundation
by royal charter of Henry VIII in 1518, the RCP
has built up magnificent collections of books,
manuscripts, portraits, silver, and medical
artefacts.
Admission FREE
www.rcplondon.ac.uk/museum-and-garden

Royal Institution
London W1
The Royal Institution is an independent charity
dedicated to connecting people with the world
of science. In the museum you can explore the
world-changing science that's happened at the
RI since 1799.
The stuff of science is woven throughout the
entire building.
Admission FREE
www.rigb.org

Interesting Facts
Royal Institution and Marie Currie
Marie & Pierre Curie are famous for their pioneering research on radioactivity. Marie Curie was the first woman to win a Nobel Prize.

In 1903 Marie & Pierre were invited to the Royal Institution in London to give a speech on radioactivity; however being female Marie was prevented from speaking, and Pierre gave the speech.

St Bartholomew's Hospital Museum
Smithfield London EC1
Set in the historic North Wing of St Bartholomew's Hospital, the Museum tells the story of this renowned institution, celebrates its achievements and explains its place in history. The Museum exhibits original and facsimile archives dating back to the 12th century.
Admission FREE
www.bartsandthelondon.nhs.uk/about-us/museums

Thrifty Tip
St Bartholomew's
The hospital run tours that take in the church of St Bartholomew the Less; the Hospital's Square, North Wing and Great Hall (all designed by James Gibbs); and Hogarth's famous biblical paintings. Tours take place every Friday see website for full details:
Admission FREE
www.bartsandthelondon.nhs.uk/about-us/museums

St Johns Ambulance Museum
Clerkenwell London EC1
The Museum covers the ancient Order's unique blend of religious, military and medical history. The Museum occupies two sites St John's Gate, and the Priory Church of St John with its surviving twelfth century Crypt.
Admission FREE
www.museumstjohn.org.uk

Interesting Fact
St Johns Ambulance
St John Ambulance is a common name used by a number of affiliated organizations in different countries dedicated to the teaching and practice of medical first aid.

* Thrifty Tip
FREE Events
St Johns Ambulance Museum
FREE Events throughout the year including Craft Activities, Creative writing workshops, Talks and Tours see website.
www.museumstjohn.org.uk

Interesting Fact
Medical Inventions
Sir Ronald Ross discovered that malaria was carried by mosquitos; this discovery laid the foundations for curing the disease. He was awarded the Nobel Peace Prize in 1902.

Military Museums

* Household Cavalry Museum
London SW1
The Household Cavalry Museum has amassed an outstanding collection of rare and unique treasures from ceremonial uniforms, royal standards and gallantry awards to musical instruments, horse furniture and silverware by Fabergé.
Admission Children and Concessions: £4.00
Adults £6.00
www.householdcavalrymuseum.co.uk

Interesting Facts
Household Cavalry Museum
The Household Cavalry Museum is a living museum about real people doing a real job in a real place. Through a large glazed partition you can see troopers working with horses in the original 18th century stables.

The Household Cavalry Museum sits within Horse Guards in Whitehall, one of the city's most historic buildings dating from 1750.

* Thrifty Tip
Household Cavalry Museum
FREE Craft Activities
The Museum runs Craft Activities based on the history and fascinating stories of the Household Cavalry, suitable for 5-11 years it starts at 11.30am for approx 45 minutes.
Children FREE with fee paying adult.
See website:
www.householdcavalrymuseum.co.uk

* Inns of Court & City Yeomany Museum
London WC2

A small collection housed in a classical George III building (dating from 1774) in Lincoln's Inn records the most unusual history of the Regiment and its predecessor units going back to 1584 when the members (all lawyers) were formed to defend London against the threat of invasion.

Admission FREE
www.armymuseums.org.uk/museums

Firepower Royal Artillery Museum
Woolwich SE18

The Museum is packed with weapons and vehicles from the 20th Century: anti-aircraft, anti-tank, coastal defence, light and medium artillery, self propelled guns and missile launchers. The Museum also has one of the largest and most comprehensive collections of Orders, Decorations and Medals, awarded to the men and women of the British Armed Forces.

Admission Child £2.50 Concessions £4.60
 Adult £5.30
www.firepower.org.uk

* Interesting Fact
Arsenal Football Club at Woolwich

Arsenal Football Club originally started at Woolwich, it dates from 1886 when a group of workers from the Woolwich firm, Royal Arsenal founded the team. The firm was an armaments factory, hence the nickname the team later acquired: "The Gunners".

Imperial War Museum
London SE1
IWM is unique in its coverage of conflicts, especially those involving Britain and the Commonwealth. They seek to provide for, and to encourage, the study and understanding of the history of modern war and wartime experience.
Admission FREE
www.iwm.org.uk

* Imperial War Museum
Horrible Histories Spies
Uncover the world of spies at this major new interactive exhibition for families. It brings the horrible history of the Second World War spies and their secrets to life, based on Terry Deary's book and the bestselling *Horrible Histories* series. Charges apply see website:
www.iwm.org.uk

Interesting Fact
Imperial War Museum
Outside the Museum you will find a section of the Berlin Wall.

* Tibetan Peace Garden
Imperial War Museum
The Tibetan Peace Garden at the museum is another highlight it is particularly pleasant to visit during springtime when the blossom is on the trees.
Admission FREE
www.iwm.org.uk

* The Guards Museum
London SW1
The museum contains a wealth of information and artefacts relating to the five regiments of Foot Guards namely Grenadier, Cold stream, Scots, Irish and Welsh Guards. You will see items relating to The Grand Old Duke of York, The Duke of Wellington, Field Marshal Alexander, and many other items.
Admission Concessions £2.50 Adults £5
Under 16s FREE
www.theguardsmuseum.com

National Army Museum
Chelsea London SW3
The National Army Museum is a leading authority on the history of the British Army. The Museum has also embarked on an collaborative project which aims to document and store the personal accounts, expertise and careers of the residents of the Royal Hospital Chelsea.
Admission FREE
www.nam.ac.uk

* National Maritime Museum
See the spectacular story of the Thames brought to life in Royal River. Explore the collection including the uniform Nelson wore at the Battle of Trafalgar. You can also steer a ship into port and fire a cannon in the Maritime galleries.
Admission FREE
www.rmg.co.uk

Royal Fusiliers Museum London EC3

The Fusilier Museum tells the story of a British infantry regiment, raised at the Tower of London in 1685. The museum follows the Regiment from its formation to the present day. **Admission FREE with entry to the Tower of London**
www.fusiliermuseumlondon.org

Thrifty Tip
Royal Fusiliers Museum
Tower Hamlets residence can visit for £1

The London Scottish Military Museum London SW1

The London Scottish Regimental Museum is located on the two balconies in the drill hall at Regimental Headquarters. Because the museum is located in a MOD building viewing is by appointment only with the Curator on Tuesdays, Wednesdays, and Thursdays, from 11.00am to 4.00pm see website:
www.londonscottishregt.org

Music Museums

Christ Church Spitalfields London

Christ Church has a stunning organ by famous organ builder Richard Bridge. The organ was installed in the church in 1735 and is considered to be the masterpiece of the greatest organ builder in Georgian England. The church has limited opening check website for details:
www.christchurchspitalfields.org

Handel House Museum London W1
Home to the great baroque composer George
Frideric Handel. He lived here from 1723 until
his death in 1759, and composed some of the
greatest music in history, including *Messiah*,
and *Music for the Royal Fireworks.*
Admission Concessions £5.00 adults £6.00
Adults Children £2.00
**Admission FREE for Children on Saturdays
and Sundays**
www.handelhouse.org

Interesting Facts
Handel House Museum
Jimmi Hendrix (regularly voted the greatest rock
guitarist), lived at Handle House with his
English girlfriend, Kathy Etchingham for two
years from1968.

Handel House Museum invites musicians
wanting to rehearse repertoire from the baroque
period to apply to use the Rehearsal and
Performance Room.

Thrifty Tip
George Fredric Handel and
The Foundling Museum
The Foundling Museum also houses the Gerald
Coke Handel Collection which is one of the
largest privately-owned collections of Handel
memorabilia.
www.foundlingmuseum.org.uk

Musical Museum
Brentford Middx

The MM Brentford contains one of the world's most comprehensive collections of automatic instruments. From the tiny clockwork musical box to the "Mighty Wurlitzer". There is also an impressive collection of Pianos, Organs, Violins and more.
Concessions £6.50 Adults £8
Admission FREE for under 16s Concessions £6.50 Adults £8
www.musicalmuseum.co.uk

Thrifty Tip
Musical Museum
The Musical Museum has an upstairs theatre complete with orchestra pit.
www.musicalmuseum.co.uk

National Sound Archive
British Library
London NW1
The British Library Sound Archive holds many sound and video recordings, with over a million discs and thousands of tapes.
Its collections come from all over the world and cover the entire range of recorded sound from music, drama and literature, to oral history and wildlife sounds. Formats range from cylinders made in the late 19th century to the latest digital media.
Admission FREE
www.bl.uk/reshelp/bldept/soundarch/about/soundarchive.html

Interesting Fact
National Sound Archive
British Library

The British Library Sounds website provides free online access for UK higher and further education institutions to over 50,000 rare recordings of music, spoken word, and human and natural environments. Many of these recordings are also accessible for general public listening online.
http://sounds.bl.uk

Royal Academy of Music Museum
London NW1
The Museum displays material from the Academy's world-renowned collection of instruments, manuscripts, objects and images. An integral part of Academy life.
Admission FREE
www.ram.ac.uk/museum

Interesting Fact
Royal Academy of Music Museum
Many of the collections are named after the individuals who collected or donated them, such as the conductor Henry Wood pianist Harriet Cohen, the concert agent Norman McCann, composer Arthur Sullivan and jazz star Kenny Wheeler.

* Thrifty Tip
Royal Academy of Music Museum
The museum regularly hosts exhibitions and events including daily live demonstrations on their historic pianos.

Royal College of Music Museum
London SW7
The RCM Museum is full of musical treasures dating from the 15th century onwards. On display you will find highlights from the collection of over 1,000 instruments including the earliest surviving stringed keyboard instrument, plus trombones owned and played by Elgar and Holst.
Admission FREE
www.rcm.ac.uk/visit/museum

Interesting Fact
Edward Elgar
Elgar is probably best known for his *Pomp and circumstance Marches..* He wrote the music to the British patriotic song *Land of Hope and Glory* which is played every year at The BBC Proms at The Royal Albert Hall.

Thrifty Tip
Royal College of Music
FREE lunchtime recitals at various locations throughout London see website:
www.rcm.ac.uk

Royal Military School of Music Museum
London
Kneller Hall is recognized as the home of Army music since its foundation in 1857.
Limited opening and booking by prior arrangement – see website
Admission FREE
www.army.mod.uk/music/23271.aspx

Interesting Fact
Royal Military School of Music Museum
The 17th Century Portrait Painter Sir Godfrey Kneller built the mansion that now houses the museum.
www.army.mod.uk/music/23271.aspx

Royal Albert Hall London SW7
The Royal Albert Hall was built to fulfil the vision of Prince Albert (Queen Victoria's consort) of a 'Central Hall' that would be used to promote understanding and appreciation of the Arts and Sciences.
Many world class performances are held at the RAH including the BBC Proms.

Interesting Fact
Royal Albert Hall
The Beatles & the Rolling Stones appeared on the same bill only once. It was at The Royal Albert Hall in 1963 and it was a gig for charity.

Thrifty Tip
Royal Albert Hall
The Proms
The BBC Proms at The RAH has the popular tradition of Promming (standing in the Arena or Gallery areas of the RAH) it is central to the unique atmosphere. Up to 1,400 standing places are available for each Proms concert. The traditionally low prices allow you to enjoy world-class performances for just £5.00 each. Promming places are available on the door see website for details.
www.royalalberthall.com

Royal Opera House London
The Royal Opera House is the home of The
Royal Opera, and The Royal Ballet.
The Royal Opera House holds many exhibitions
throughout the year, backstage tours are also
available.
**Admission FREE (for many of the
exhibitions)**
www.roh.org.uk

Interesting Fact
Royal Opera House
Many of Handel's operas were specifically
written for the Royal Opera House and had
their premiers there.

Thrifty Tip
Royal Opera House
£6 Tickets
Standing seats available for many performances
from as little as £6 these do need to be booked
in advance as they are very popular.

Thrifty Tip
Royal Opera House
BP FREE Summer Screenings
Do not miss London's BP Big Summer
Screenings which include relays from both
Ballet and Opera productions see ROH website
for details:
www.roh.org.uk

Salvation Army Museum of Music
London WC1
The Salvation Army heritage centre provides an
overview of the history of The Salvation Army.

Including the story of instruments, and music composers that have made the army so distinctive.
Admission FREE
www.salvationarmy.org.uk/uki/HeritageM useum

Interesting Fact
Salvation Army Museum Music
The Christian Mission (later called the Salvation Army) was founded in the East End of London in 1865 by William & Catherine Booth.

Thrifty Tip For Music Lovers
Broadgate Piano London
Broadgate has a piano situated just off Finsbury Avenue Square by Costa Coffee. Play away in a quiet and private area of Broadgate Monday to Sunday between 07:00hrs to 19:00.
www.broadgate.co.uk

Maritime Museums

* Cutty Sark London SE10
The Cutty Sark is a British Tea Clipper built at the Clyde in 1869, she was one of the fastest tea clippers ever built.
FREE to view from outside
www1.rmg.co.uk

* Golden Hinde 11 London SE1

Here you can experience Tudor life aboard the Golden Hinde II a full sized reconstruction of Sir Francis Drake's galleon. Explore this vessel which offers a unique insight into Drake's circumnavigation of the globe from. **Admission Children under 16 FREE** Concessions £4.50 Adults £6 **www.goldenhinde.com**

* National Maritime Museum

At the National Maritime Museum See the spectacular story of the Thames brought to life in Royal River. Explore the collection including the uniform Nelson wore at the Battle of Trafalgar. You can also steer a ship into port and fire a cannon in the Maritime galleries. **Admission FREE** **www.rmg.co.uk**

Postal Museums

Mount Pleasant Post Office
London EC1
The Royal Mail Archive and research centre holds the written records of Royal Mail, the GPO and the Post Office, as well as stamps, posters, photos and more. There is also a research library where you can do family history searches. **Admission FREE see website** **www.postalheritage.org.uk/page/visiting**

Thrifty Tip
Mount Pleasant Post Office
Unlike most items in the archive, to research original material in the philatelic collections you must make an appointment with the Curator of Philately
www.postalheritage.org.uk/page/visiting

* Postal Museum Store Debden Essex
The Museum collection (which includes vehicles, pillar boxes, furniture and sorting equipment) is at the British Postal Museum Store.
Visiting is by guided tour only see website for full details.
Admission FREE
www.postalheritage.org.uk

Printing Typing & Stationary Museums

St Brides Printing Workshop London EC4
St Brides is the world's foremost printing and graphic arts library. St Bride Library was opened in 1895. It was both a technical library and printing school. To this day St Bride Foundation aims to keep the tradition and heritage of printing alive through a diverse selection of workshops, lectures and conferences.
Limited opening see website:
Admission FREE
www.sbf.org.uk

Smythson Stationary Museum London W1
Small museum behind the shop packed with
stationery products including original 1902
Smythson diaries, John F Kennedy's and
Princess Grace of Monaco's condolence books,
old Christmas cards and wartime telegrams.
www.smythson.com

Type Museum London SW9
The TM has largest typographic collection in
the world. With punches, matrices and moulds
from the principal eighteenth- and nineteenth-
century London type foundries, complemented
by business archives and by one of the world's
best collections of type specimen books.

Please Note
The Museum is being developed please check
website before visiting.
www.typemuseum.org

The Stephen (INK) Collection London N3
A small museum that features the history of the
Stephens family and the eponymous ink
company, with a section on the developmen of
writing materials. Located in Avenue House the
home of Henry "Inky" Stephens from 1874
until his death.
Admission FREE
www.london-
northwest.com/sites/Stephens

Interesting Fact
Dr Henry Stephens
Dr Henry Stephens (1796–1864) was the inventor in 1832 of an indelible "blue-black writing fluid" which was to become famous as Stephens Ink.
www.avenuehouse.org.uk

Radio Telecommunication & Wireless Museums

* The British Vintage Wireless and Television Museum London SE21
The private Museum has an ever-expanding range of radios, televisions, speakers and radiograms from the dawn of radio up to the last valve model ever made.
Admission FREE
www.bvwtm.org.uk

Interesting Fact
The British Vintage Wireless and TV Museum
The property housing the museum has had a rich heritage of radio and electricity. Alfred Rickard-Taylor (an early wireless enthusiast) lived here from 1908 to 1914.
www.bvwtm.org.uk

Science & Zoology Museums

* Astronomy Centre Greenwich SE10

Astronomy Gallery highlights include the oldest thing you'll ever touch a 4.5 billion year-old meteorite. Watch how the universe was formed - from Big Bang to now in 4 minutes. Guide a space mission or try your hand at being an astronomer. Get answers to the big questions from the on-screen experts.

Admission FREE
www.rmg.co.uk/royal-observatory/astronomy-and-time-galleries

Meteor Showers during August in UK

Every August in the UK you can look for the Perseids Meteor Shower (shooting Stars) around August 10-13.

www.earthsky.org

* British Museum
Enlightenment Gallery London WC1

The Enlightenment was an age of reason and learning that flourished across Europe and America from about 1680 to 1820. This rich and diverse permanent exhibition uses thousands of objects to demonstrate how people in Britain understood their world during this period.

Admission FREE (Plus FREE daily Tours)
www.britishmuseum.org

* Interesting Fact
The museum is renowned for its amazing reconstructions.

* Thrifty Tip
British Museum
FREE Activities
FREE trails workshops and activities for family visits

* Grant Museum of Zoology
UCL London WC1
The Grant Museum of Zoology is the only remaining university zoological museum in London. It houses around 67,000 specimens, covering the whole Animal Kingdom. The Museum is packed full of skeletons, mounted animals and specimens preserved in fluid. Many of the species are now endangered or extinct.
Admission FREE
www.ucl.ac.uk/museums/zoology

* Thrifty Tip
Grant Museum of Zoology UCL FREE
Events & Family Activities
Many FREE events and FREE family fun days throughout the year

Interesting Fact
Robert Grant
Robert Grant a sponge expert was Darwin's most important mentor at Edinburgh. He and Darwin often went on long walks at the Firth of Forth, discussing marine biology and collecting samples.
www.ucl.ac.uk/museums/zoology

* Royal Institution of Great Britain
London W1
In the museum you can explore the world-changing science that's happened at the RI since 1799. Wherever you go in the RI you'll see the instruments that have made science work for the last two centuries. The stuff of science is woven throughout the entire building.
Admission FREE
www.rigb.org

Interesting Fact
Royal Institution
The Royal Institution is an independent charity dedicated to connecting people with the world of science. There about discovery, innovation, inspiration and imagination.

* Royal Observatory
Greenwich SE10
Home of Greenwich Mean Time (GMT) and the Prime Meridian of the World. It is also home to London's only planetarium, the Harrison timekeepers and the UK's largest refracting telescope.
Admission FREE
www.rmg.co.uk

Interesting Fact
Collapsible Telescope
The Reflecting Telescope was built by Sir Issac Newton.
www.rmg.co.uk/royal-observatory

* Science Museum
South Kensington London SW7
The Science Museum is world renowned for its
historic collections, awe-inspiring galleries and
inspirational exhibitions. The Science Museum
now holds a collection of over 300,000 items,
including such famous items as Stephenson's
Rocket the first jet engine a reconstruction of
Francis Crick and James Watson's model of
DNA.
Admission FREE
www.sciencemuseum.org.uk

* Interesting Facts
Science Museum
The Science Museum also contains over 800
interactive exhibits that science enthusiasts will
love.

* See Apollo 10 at the Science Museum, Apollo
10 was launched in May 69 on a lunar mission
as the rehearsal for the actual Apollo 11 landing.

* The Science Museum also has an IMAX
Cinema and several flight simulators - charges
are made for these.

* Science Museum FREE Exhibitions
The Science Museum also runs a program of
FREE exhibitions see website
Admission FREE
www.sciencemuseum.org.uk

Thrifty Tip for Science Lovers
Science lovers may also enjoy a visit to Down
House in Kent Charles Darwin's Home.

Down House Downe Kent
Home of Charles Darwin
Down House, the home of Charles Darwin. has
a unique place in the history of science. See the
study where Darwin wrote 'On the Origin of
Species', still as it was when he worked there,
and stroll through the extensive gardens that so
inspired the great scientist.
www.english-heritage.org.uk

* Time Gallery Flamsted House &
Meridian Courtyard Greenwich SE10
The Time Gallery looks at the historical need to
develop increasingly accurate time keeping. The
Meridian Courtyard is where you can stand on
the world-famous Greenwich Meridian Line,
which represents the Prime Meridian of the
World Longitude 0°. Every place on Earth is
measured in terms of its distance east or west
from the Greenwich Meriden.
Admission Children £2 Concession £4.50
Adults £6.35
www.rmg.co.uk/royal-
observatory/astronomy-and-time-galleries

* Interesting Fact
Meridian Line
The line itself divides the eastern and western
hemispheres of the Earth, just as the Equator
divides the northern and southern hemispheres.

231

Sport Museums

Cricket

* MCC Museum Lords Cricket Ground London NW8

The MCC Museum is both world-class and world-famous. While it contains a wide range of exhibits, it is best-known for being the home of "The Ashes". Other displays include a cricket kit used by some of the greatest players of all time. The MCC has been collecting cricketing artifacts since 1864.

Admission £5 Concessions and £7.50 Adults (does not include ground tour)

www.lords.org/fixtures/ticket-information/free-entry-to-lords

Interesting Fact
The Ashes Tour
The Ashes is a Test Cricket series played between England and Australia since 1882, it is played every two years.

Interesting Fact
WG Grace
WG Grace is perhaps the most famous cricketer of all; the Museum has displays that recognize his life and achievements with portraits, busts and other memorabilia associated with the incomparable 'W.G.'

* Lords

Lords Cricket Ground the home of MCC prides itself that cricket from all levels from Schools & Colleges (Eton V Harrow and Oxford v Cambridge Cricket is played there).

Also village games, tests and ODI's are played each summer at the home of Cricket.

* Thrifty Tip
Lords FREE Tickets
FREE tickets to a handful of fixtures are available each summer, these fixtures usually involve MCC see website for details:
www.lords.org/fixtures/ticket-information/free-entry-to-lords

* The Oval Cricket Club
Kennington SE11
The Oval is home to Surrey County Cricket Club, one of the most historic sports clubs in the UK. The club has staged International cricket since 1882. The Club Tour gives visitors the chance to discover the history of the club and the iconic stadium.
The Oval Cricket Club Tickets
Tickets can be purchased from £10
Under 16s only £1
www.kiaoval.com

Interesting Facts
The Oval
The Oval has staged International cricket since 1882, and was the ground where the Ashes were born.

The first ever FA Cup Final was played at the Oval in 1872.

Thrifty Tip for Cricket Lovers

* Since 1802 amateur Cricket has been played on Saturday at 2pm at London Fields.

Football Museums

* Arsenal FC Museum
Arsenal supporters can expect their favorite exhibitions, including Michael Thomas' boots from Anfield '89 and Charlie George's FA Final Cup shirt from 1971, along with a recently-donated array of memorabilia. There is also a customised trophy on display that was presented to the club by the FA Premier League for remaining unbeaten throughout the 2003/04 season.
Admission £4 under 16s Adults £7 (does not include ground tour).
www.arsenal.com/history/the-arsenal-museum

Interesting Fact
Arsenal Football Club
Arsenal Football Club originally started at Woolwich, it dates from 1886 when a group of workers from the Woolwich firm, Royal Arsenal founded the team. The firm was an armaments factory, hence the nickname the team later acquired: "The Gunners".

* Thrifty Tip
Islington Museum
Arsenal Exhibition 2013
The Islington Museum Arsenal Exhibition celebrating 100 years of AFC playing in Islington.
www.arsenal.com/history/the-arsenal-museum

* Chelsea FC Museum
The Chelsea Museum gives you the chance to see how Chelsea has evolved on and off the pitch to become one of the greatest football clubs in the world. It offers a highly interactive experience, bringing the club's past alive through audio visual shows as well as a fascinating collection of Chelsea related memorabilia. Also see some of the most iconic images from the club's history.
Child £8 Concession £9
www.chelseafc.com/museum

* West Ham United FC London E13
West Ham United have thrown open the doors to a new museum tracing the club's history from shipbuilding and the '66 World Cup to the Premier League.
Admission Children under 5 FREE
Concessions £4 Adults £6
www.whufc.com

Interesting Fact
West Ham United FC
The club was founded in 1895 as Thames Ironworks FC.

It was named after the company whose employees were its first players and its links with the shipbuilding industry. Thames Ironworks FC reformed in 1900 as West Ham United.
www.whufc.com

Rugby

* Rugby Football Union Museum Twickenham
The World Rugby Museum has the oldest, most extensive and important collection of rugby football memorabilia in the world. The collection includes over 10,000 objects, 7000 pieces of archival material and between 7-8000 photographs.
Admission Concessions £5 Adults £7 (prices do not include stadium tour)
www.rfu.com/twickenhamstadium/worldru gbymuseum

Interesting Fact
World Rugby Museum Archive
The World Rugby Museum archive and collections are available to researchers and scholars to view upon appointment. Please contact the museum to make arrangements.
0208 892 8877

Theatre Museums

* Victoria & Albert Theatre Museum

The Theatre and Performance collection at the
V&A was founded in the 1920s when a private
collector, Gabrielle Enthoven, donated her
extensive collection of theatrical designs,
memorabilia, books and photographs to the
Museum. Since then the collection has
continued to grow and has costumes (some that
can be tried on), Props, Screens.

*Performances

Prformances take place at the Theatre Museum
including a performance of The Lion King.
www.vam.ac.uk/page/t/theatre-and-performance

Interesting Fact

Jane Pritchard who wrote the book *Pavlova
Twentieth Century Ballerina* is Curator of
Dance at the V&A.

Transport Railway & Steam Museums

* Kew Museum of Steam

The heart of the museum is its collection of
magnificent steam pumping engines. These
comprise the Cornish engines, and the rotative
engines, which have been collected by the
museum trust from pumping stations across the
country.

Together the collection demonstrates the major developments in steam engine technology.
Admission Children £4 Concessions £9.00
www.kbsm.org

* London Transport Museum London Covent Garden WC2
London Transport Museum celebrates the past and present and future of London Transport. The Museum's collection originated in the 1920s, when the London General Omnibus Company decided to preserve two Victorian horse buses and an early motorbus for future generations.
Concessions £11.50 Adults £13.50 and tickets allow unlimited entry
for a whole year.
Admission FREE for TfL staff TfL nominee's and children under 16
www.ltmuseum.co.uk

* Markfield Beam Engine & Museum Tottenham London N17
The Markfield Beam Engine and Museum site consists of the remains of the Tottenham sewage treatment works and pumping station. The works were operational for over one hundred years. Features include the remains of the walls of the original settlement tanks and filter beds and the original pump houses, one of which contains the Beam Pumping Engine.
Limited opening see website for details:
Admission FREE
www.mbeam.org

* **Walthamstow Pump house Museum London E17**
Today the museum is home to a growing collection of transport artefacts and displays, interpreting the nationally important steam and transport first achievements.
Admission FREE most Sundays see website www.walthamstowpumphousemuseum.org. uk/visit.html

* **Thrifty Tip FREE Events**
Walthamstow Pump house Museum also runs a series of events many of which are FREE

* **Whitewebbs Museum of Transport Enfield Middx**
Home to a collection of old vehicles including motorbikes and classic cars, it also has a collection of industrial vehicles including old delivery vans, and fire engines, and a model railway. Limited opening - see website
Admission Adults £4.00
Admission FREE for Children accompanied by an adult.
www.whitewebbsmuseum.co.uk

Thrifty Tips for Steam Train Lovers

* **Chingford Model Steam Train Chingford E4**
The railways are used to give rides to members of the public on the Model Steam Trains.

239

Open Sundays and Bank Holiday Monday afternoons between April and the end of September from 2pm - 5:30pm.
Prices 50p for the raised track, £1 for the ground level track see website:
www.chingford-model-engineering.com

* Epping Ongar Heritage Railway
Step back in time and experience the romance of steam travel in bygone times while passing through picturesque countryside, beautiful forest and historic towns. Tickets allow you unlimited travel all day long.
Children (3-16) £7
Concessions £11
Adults £13
Children under 3 FREE
http://eorailway.co.uk

Windmill Museums

* Brixton Windmill Museum
London SW12
Brixton Windmill is a tangible reminder to all Londoners of the close links that the capital had with agriculture and food production.
Admission FREE
www.brixtonwindmill.org/home

Interesting Fact
Brixton Windmill
In May 2013 Brixton Windmill unveiled its new MURAL, in the children's garden

* Thrifty Tip
**Brixton Windmill Museum FREE Tours &
Events**
FREE Daily tours available plus FREE Events
throughout the summer.
FREE Christmas party – see website:
www.brixtonwindmill.org/home

* Windmill Museum
Wimbledon London SW19
The museum has exhibits for the young and
old, covering windmills and milling as well as
local history and the Scouting movement. There
is interest for all ages.
Admission Concessions & Children £1 Adults
£2
www.wimbledonwindmill.org.uk

Interesting Fact
Windmill Museum
Wimbledon
The Windmill Museum was once the home of
Lord Baden-Powell founder of the Boy Scout
Movement. It is here that he wrote parts of
Scouting for Boys in 1908.

Museums Other

* Benjamin Franklin House Museum
London WC2
Benjamin Franklin House is the world's only
remaining Franklin home. For nearly sixteen
years between 1757 and 1775, Dr Benjamin
Franklin scientist, diplomat, philosopher,
inventor, Founding Father of the United States
lived behind its doors. Built circa 1730, it is

today a dynamic museum and educational
facility.
Admission Concession £5 Adult £7
Admission FREE for under 16s
www.benjaminfranklinhouse.org

Thrifty Tips
Benjamin Franklin House
Visit FREE During Open House London
FREE to visit during Open House weekend see
Open House website:
www.londonopenhouse.org

* Benjamin Franklin House
FREE Events
Many FREE events take place in the house
throughout the year see website. There is also
the Annual Friends and Neighbours Christmas
Party where you can celebrate the festive season
in the great British holiday tradition, enjoy a
mince pie and a glass or two of homemade
mulled wine.

* Interesting Fact
Benjamin Franklin and
St Bartholomew-the-Great
The Lady Chapel at St Bartholomew the great
had been previously used for commercial
purposes and it was there that Benjamin
Franklin served a year as journeyman printer.

* Brunel Museum
Thames Tunnel London SE16
The Brunel Museum commemorates the work
of Father & Son Marc Isambard Brunel and
Isambard Kingdom Brunel.

The Engine House Exhibition tells the story of the building of the Thames Tunnel by Marc and his son Isambard Kingdom Brunel.
Admission Concession £1.50 Adults £3
www.brunel-museum.org.uk

* Interesting Facts
Floodlit Brunel Tunnel Tours
Floodlit Brunel Tunnel Tours also arranged see website for details:
www.brunel-museum.org.uk

Isambard Kingdom Brunel's
London Home
If you are a fan of Brunel you may like to visit his former home in London at 98 Cheyne Walk Chelsea London SW10, and Hungerford Bridge designed by Brunel, and Paddington Station.

Burgh House and Hampstead Museum
New End Square NW3
This beautiful grade I listed Georgian building houses the Hampstead Museum which has an interesting collection of exhibits on the history of the local area.
Admission FREE
www.burghhouse.org.uk/museum

Interesting Fact
Burgh House and Hampstead Museum
The Museum holds largest archive and collection of Helen Allingham (one of the finest watercolour artists of Victorian times) material in the world.

* Canal Museum Kings Cross London N1

At the London Canal Museum you can see inside a narrow boat cabin, learn about the history of London's canals, about the cargoes carried, the people who lived and worked on the waterways, and the horses that pulled their boats.

Admission Children £2 Concession £3
Adult £4

www.canalmuseum.org.uk

* Clockmakers Museum/Guildhall Library London EC2

The Clockmakers' Museum collection is housed in the Guildhall Library. It is the oldest collection specifically of clocks and watches in the world, with about 1,000 exhibits.

Admission FREE
www.cityoflondon.gov.uk

* Clowns Gallery Holy Trinity Church Museum London E8

The church known also as" The Clowns Church" has a small Clowns Museum it is open to the public on the first Friday of the month. There is a display of photographs depicting various aspects of clowning and its history and a picture gallery. Various small items are displayed in show cases and there is the Grimaldi Corner altar.

www.trinitysaintsunited.com

Interesting Fact
Clowns Memorial Service

An annual Clowns memorial service is held at Holy Trinity church to pay tribute to Joseph

Grimaldi, the founder of the modern clown, who died in 1837.

* Thrifty Tip
Memorial Day
Joseph Grimaldi Park London N1
Joseph Grimaldi Memorial Day is an annual event that celebrates the life of Joseph Grimaldi. A tribute will be held at Grimaldi's grave followed by various events throughout the day see website for full details:
www.clowns-international.com

Interesting Fact
Joseph Grimaldi made his debut at Sadlers Wells aged just 3 years.

Cumming Museum London SE13
The Cuming Museum is the home of the worldwide collection of the Cuming Family and the museum of Southwark's history. The Victorian father and son team, Richard and Henry Cuming loved collecting weird and unusual objects and the Museum houses a diverse collection that includes archaeology, ethnography, social history and natural history, and it is an art lover's haven.
Admission FREE
www.southwark.gov.uk/cumingmuseum

Thrifty Tip
Cumming Museum
The Museum of Southwark is also in the Cumming Museum Building.

Denis Severs' House London E1

A Grade II listed Georgian terraced house in Spitalfields From 1979 to 1999 it was lived in by Dennis Severs a Canadian Artist, who gradually recreated the rooms as a time capsule in the style of former centuries mainly from the 18th and 19th centuries. A must visit for anyone who loves Art & Design.
www.dennissevershouse.co.uk

Thrifty Tip
Denis Severs' House
Visit on Mondays Lunchtimes between 12pm-2pm for just £7.

* Discover Greenwich London

At the Discover Greenwich Visitor Centre you can explore over 500 years of history through a fascinating permanent exhibition. The permanent exhibition, which includes historical artifacts, scale models, film footage and hands-on displays, tells the story of the people who shaped the buildings and landscape of Greenwich through the centuries.
Admission FREE
www.ornc.org/visit/attractions/discover-greenwich-visitor-centre

Interesting Fact
ORNC Greenwich
The remains of one of Henry's VIII favourite palaces lie just a few feet below the ORNC site. More than 30 objects excavated on site allow you to picture the splendour of the Tudor palace.

Fan Museum London SE10

The Fan Museum is the first and only museum in the world devoted in its entirety to all aspects of the ancient art and craft of the fan. It has been described as "an architectural and artistic gem", and as "an oasis of tranquillity".
Admission FREE for OAPs and Disabled on Tuesday from 2pm.
www.thefanmuseum.org.uk

Thrifty Tip
Fan Museum Afternoon Tea

Afternoon Tea is served Tuesdays and Sundays in the Museums beautiful orangery. Afternoon Tea is £6 per person and includes Tea/Coffee, Scones Cream and Jam, and Homemade Cakes Booking recommended.
www.thefanmuseum.org.uk

Interesting Fact
The Fan Museum Orangery

The Orangery is decorated with a beautiful mural by Jane Barraclough which gives the room a wonderful atmosphere, and it overlooks a 'secret' garden in the Japanese manner, with a fan shaped parterre, pond, stream and oriental architectural features.

Fenton House Museum
Hampstead
London NW3

The great poet John Keats lived here from 1818 to 1820 until he travelled to Rome and died of tuberculosis, aged just 25. The house has been restored as a museum with period decor, furnishings and a collection of Keatsiana.

In the grounds is the Heath Library which has a great collection of local books and periodicals, and provides free internet access - Admission Child £3 Adults £6.
www.nationaltrust.org.uk/fenton-house

* Thrifty Tip
Foundling Museum
FREE Drop in Activities and Concerts
FREE Drop in activities for children and families, also FREE concerts and events see website for full details
www.foundlingmuseum.org.uk

Freud Museum Hampstead London NW3
The home of Sigmund Freud and his family when they escaped from the Nazi's in Austria in 1938. The centrepiece of the museum is Freud's study it also contains Freud's remarkable collection of antiquities Egyptian, Greek, Roman and Oriental. The walls are lined with shelves containing Freud's large library.
Admission Concessions £3.00 Adults £6
Admission under 12s FREE
www.freud.org.uk

Fulham Palace Museum London SW6
The beautiful Tudor Fulham Palace was at one time the main residence of the Bishop of London. The Museum Collection includes paintings, archaeology and artefacts, as well as the Palace itself, as demonstrated by a fascinating scale model of the building.
Admission FREE
www.fulhampalace.org

* Fulham Palace Museum
FREE Workshops and Drop in Sessions
Many FREE workshops for families and adults
throughout the year – see website:
www.fulhampalace.org

Goldsmiths Hall London EC2
A changing display of antique and modern silver
selected from the Collections is displayed during
the year within the Hall.
Only open during exhibitions see website for
full details.
Admission FREE
www.thegoldsmiths.co.uk

Gunnersbury Park Museum London W3
The museum was opened in 1929 as a Museum
of social History. It has collected a wide range
of objects, paintings and photographs which
reflect life in Ealing and Hounslow Boroughs
from prehistory to the present day. It still
continues to collect material to make sure that
visitors in the future will be able to see how we
lived today.
Admission FREE
www.hounslow.info

* Interesting Fact
Gunnersbury Park
Gunnersbury Park was a former home of the
Rothchilds family, visitors can see carriages that
were once owned by the Rothchild family. Also
at weekends visitors can visit the family's
Victorian kitchen.

Hackney Museum London E8
The museum tells the story of Hackney's past
and present through special exhibitions,
permanent displays and special community
exhibitions produced with local partners.
Admission FREE
www.hackney.gov.uk/hackney-museum

Hogarth House Chiswick London W4
Hogarth House was the country home of the
great painter William Hogarth. Hogarth's talents
and interests were wide-ranging, and displays in
the house tell the story of his life at the house.
Several of Hogarth's paintings are on view in
the house.
Admission FREE
www.hounslow.info

Interesting Fact
William Hogarth
William Hogarth hated injustice snobbery and
pretension and deplored the degradation
suffered by the poor. He was a supporter of the
Foundling Children's Home, and some of his
works can be seen at the Foundling Museum.

* Horniman Museum London SE23
The Horniman Museum and Gardens, an
inspiring, surprising, family-friendly, attraction
in South London. With Anthropology, Musical
Instruments and Natural History collections
displayed in six free galleries.with an acclaimed
Aquarium and award-winning Gardens.
Admission FREE
www.horniman.ac.uk

Thrifty Tips
Horniman Museum

* FREE Aquarium
Take a magical journey through rivers, seas and oceans in the Horniman's highly acclaimed Aquarium.

* Horniman Museum
FREE Activities
FREE Activities, including creative play, enchanting stories from around the world, simple art and craft, songs and a whole lot of fun.

Horniman Museum Gardens
The Gardens have amazing sundials and great views of London.

Horniman Museum Lates
Themed after-hours events for adult visitors. Admission from £3.

* House Mill London E3
The House Mill is a grade 1 listed 18th century tidal mill set in a beautiful riverside location in the heart of London's East End, originally built in 1776. The Miller's House next door provides a visitor, information, and education centre. Visits are by guided tours: Concessions £1.50, Adults £3
Admission FREE for Children (accompanied by an adult)
www.housemill.org.uk

Jewish Museum London NW1

The Museum reflects the diverse roots and social history of Jewish people across London, including the experiences of refugees from Nazism. It also developed an acclaimed programme of Holocaust and anti-racist education.

Admission Child (5-16) £3.50 Concessions £6.50 Adults £7.50

www.jewishmuseum.org.uk

Interesting Fact
Jewish Museum
Amy Winehouse Exhibition

The Jewish Museum is staging an original exhibition about Amy Winehouse, co-curated with her brother Alex and sister-in-law Riva. It is an intimate and moving exhibition about a much loved sister. The family has given the Jewish Museum unprecedented access to Amy's personal belongings that celebrate her passion for music, fashion, suduko, Snoopy, London and her family.

Linley Sambourne House Museum
London W8

A Victorian row house built in the classic Italianate style and purchased in 1874 by Edward Linley Sambourne (Punch Cartoonist). Sambourne and his wife lived in the house for 36 years. Their son lived in the home until he died in 1946. It then passed to the daughter who preserved it intact.

Admission Prices Concessions £6 Adults £7

www.rbkc.gov.uk

Interesting Fact
Linley Sambourne
Edward Linley Sambourne was the ancestor of
Lord Snowdon husband of Princess Margaret.

London Motorbike Museum
London Greenford
The LMM is London's only motorcycle
museum it is the capital's friendly focus for
Britain's biking history and heritage. There is
over 100 machines and other exhibits on
permanent display plus a knowledgeable staff
with personal insights and stories.
Children £1.00 OAP's £2.50 Adults £5.00
Under 5yrs FREE Adults £5.00
www.london-motorcycle-museum.org

London Sewing Machine Museum
London SW17
The Museum has over 1000 machines and is
open first Saturday of every month only.
Tel 0208 682 7916
Admission FREE

London Silvers Vaults London EC2
The London Silver Vaults is the world's largest
retailer of antique Silver, and an interesting and
exciting place to visit. They have exhibitions
throughout the year.
See website for details:
www.thesilvervaults.com/news

* Mansion House London EC4
The official residence of the Lord Mayor of
London.

Built in the age of Hogarth, the Mansion House is a rare surviving Georgian town palace in central London. Highlights include The Egyptian Hall a grand room, based on designs by the classical Roman architect Vitruvius. Every Tuesday at 2pm you may visit the building as part of the tour
See website for details:
Admission Concessions £5 Adults £7
www.cityoflondon.gov.uk

* Thrifty Tip
Mansion House
FREE During Open House Weekend
Visit Mansion House FREE of charge as part of Open House Architectural Festival.
Annual Event September
See website
www.londonopenhouse.org

Museum of Immigration
Spitalfields London E1
A magical unrestored Huguenot master silk weaver's home, whose shabby frontage conceals a rare surviving synagogue built over its garden. The Museum is currently too fragile to permanently welcome the public; there is limited open days see website for full details.
Admission FREE
www.19princeletstreet.org.uk

Museum of Methodism and
John Wesley's House London EC1
The Museum of Methodism was opened in 1984 in the Crypt of Wesley's Chapel.

The museum holds one of the world's largest collections of Wesleyan ceramics and some of the finest Methodist paintings. Visitors can step back in time and stand in Wesley's original pulpit from The Foundry Chapel.
Admission FREE
www.wesleyschapel.org.uk/museum.htm

Thrifty Tip
Museum of Methodism
FREE Thursday Conversations & Services that attract speakers who are prominent in public life, from the arts, journalism, faith groups, politics, science, entertainment and of course the whole breadth of the Christian Church.

National Archives Museum
Keepers Gallery
Kew
The interactive museum showcases the treasures of the archives, featuring over 1,000 years of history. The exhibition traces the history of The National Archives and record keeping. Limited opening.
Admission FREE
www.nationalarchives.gov.uk

* Thrifty Tip
Doomsday Book Exhibition at Kew
The Doomsday Book is a record of the great survey of much of England & Wales completed in 1086. There is a new rotating exhibit in the central part of the museum that will feature Doomsday for approximately six months every five years.

* Thrifty Tip
National Archives
FREE Events
FREE Events include public talks on records of
interest, to training courses for archivists and
academics.

Queens House Museum Greenwich SE10
The 17th-century Queen's House represents a
turning point in English architecture. It was
originally the home of Charles I's queen,
Henrietta Maria. It now showcases the
Museum's outstanding fine art collection.
Admission FREE
www.rmg.co.uk

* Ragged School Museum London E3
Housed in what was once London's biggest
Ragged School, this popular, family-friendly
museum welcomes people of all ages to taste a
slice of Victorian life.
Admission FREE
www.raggedschoolmuseum.org.uk

* Interesting Fact
Ragged School Museum
On the first Sunday of every month a Victorian
lesson is re-enacted

* Thrifty Tip
Ragged School Museum
The Museum also offers, through role-play,
hands-on exhibits and talks, an authentic and
memorable experience of the poor of the East
End a century ago.

Open between 10am and 5pm each Wednesday & Thursday or between 2pm and 5pm on the first Sunday of each month.

**Rudolf Steiner House Museum
London NW1**
The General Anthroposophical Society founded by Rudolf Steiner. Rudolf Steiner gave many insights to help us to get to grips with the world we live in and to equip us to meet what is coming towards us. Rudolf Steiner House run a series of exhibitions events and workshops see website for full details:
www.rsh.anth.org.uk

**Thrifty Tip
Rudolf Steiner House
Lectures**
The insights lecture series are on Tuesdays & Fridays
Admission Concessions Students and under 25s
£1 Adults £3.50
www.rsh.anth.org.uk

Salvation Army Museum London WC1
The Salvation Army heritage centre provides an overview of the history of The Salvation Army its heritage and its work. It also includes the story of the instruments, music, composers and musicians that have made the Army so distinctive.
**Admission FREE
www.salvationarmy.org.uk/uki/HeritageM
useum**

Interesting Fact
Salvation Army
The Christian Mission was founded in the East
End of London in 1865 by William & Catherine
Booth; in 1868 the Mission changed its name to
the Salvation Army.

Savoy Hotel Museum London WC2
The Savoy Hotel has a small museum next to
the American Bar, it displays some interesting
information and paraphernalia from the hotel's
history. Exhibits include a first edition of Harry
Craddock's Savoy Cocktail Book, Noel
Coward's lighter and cigarette case and Marlene
Dietrich's guest card showing her request for 12
pink roses and a bottle of Dom Perpignan.
Admission FREE
www.fairmont.com/savoy-london

Interesting Fact
Savoy Hotel
The Savoy Hotel was built by impresario
Richard D'Oyly Cartes profits from his Gilbert
& Sullivan operas.

Interesting Fact
Savoy Court
This private road (which is the approach to the
Savoy Hotel) is the only road in London where
drivers drive on the right.

* Sherlock Holmes Museum
Baker Steet London W1
Sherlock Holmes lived at Baker Street 1881-
1904 according to the stories written by Sir
Arthur Conan Doyle.

The 1st floor study is still faithfully maintained for posterity as it was kept in Victorian Times. Admission Concessions £5 Adults £8
www.sherlock-holmes.co.uk

Soseki Museum London SW4
A private terraced house, now converted into a museum. Japan's most distinguished novelist lived here from 1900 to 1902.
http://soseki.intlcafe.info/j-menu.html

Southside House London SW19
Described by connoisseurs as an unforgettable experience Southside House provides an enchantingly eccentric backdrop to the lives and loves of generations of the Pennington Mellor Munthe families.
Re-fashioned in the William and Mary style, behind the long façade are the old rooms with a superb collection of art and historical objects reflecting centuries of ownership and style. Admission Students £6.00
www.southsidehouse.com/pages/aboutsouthsideho.html

Interesting Fact
Southside House
John Pennington's great granddaughter Hilda married Axel Munthe, the charismatic Swedish doctor whose most famous book, The Story of St Michele which is amongst the ten best sellers of the 20th century.

St Brides Church Crypt Museum London EC4

When you enter this church, you are walking in the footsteps of Kings and Queens, princes of the Church, leaders of State and famous men and women of literature and history. The crypt museum has details of the history going back to roman times.

There is also a Roman pavement and mosaic in the crypt.

www.stbrides.com

* Thrifty Tip
St Brides
FREE Lunchtime Recitals
Music plays an enormous and vital role in the life of St Bride's. Central to this is the work of the professional choir of 12 adult singers, which sings at morning and evening services every Sunday throughout the year
www.stbrides.com

Strawberry Hill Twickenham TW1
Horace Walpole's Stunning White Gothic Castle is one of England's most elegant and eccentric Gothic houses. Magically lit by a unique collection of renaissance glass, its gloomy castle-like hall and grey gothic staircase lead dramatically to the magnificence of the gallery.
www.strawberryhillhouse.org.uk

Thrifty Tips
Strawberry Hill
FREE to vist during Open House
See website for future participation and dates:
www.londonopenhouse.org

Strawberry Hill
Walpole's garden with its winding paths grove of trees, lilacs, honeysuckles is a riot of informality.
Admission to garden Student £5
www.strawberryhillhouse.org.uk

* The Thames Barrier London SE18
The magnificent Thames Barrier is the world's second-largest movable flood barrier. The barrier was designed by Rendel, Palmer and Tritton. Its purpose is to prevent London from being flooded by exceptionally high tides and surges moving up from the sea. The barrier spans 520 metres across the River Thames near Woolwich.
Admission Concessions £3.25 Adults £3.75
www.environment-agency.gov.uk

* Tower Bridge Exhibition London SE1
Enjoy stunning views of London from the high level walkways and continue your journey to the Victorian Engine Rooms to learn about the inner workings of the Most Famous Bridge in the World.
Admission Children £3.40 Concessions £5.60 Adults £8
www.towerbridge.org.uk

* Trinity Buoy Lighthouse
London E14
The iconic Experimental Lighthouse and its neighbour the Chain and Buoy Store were built by Douglass in 1864.

They were in constant use to test maritime lighting equipment and train lighthouse keepers.
www.trinitybuoywharf.com

Interesting Fact
Trinity Buoy
The roof space adjoining the present lighthouse housed the workshop for the famous scientist Michael Faraday.

* Interesting Fact
Time & Tide Bell Trinity Wharf
The Time & Tide Bell is located on the Thames side of the river wall, it's the brainchild of Sculptor Marcus Vergette, this eye-catching 3 metre double bell is the third in a planned series of 12 bells at widespread locations throughout the UK. The bell is rung by the river to mark each high tide.

* The Vault Hard Rock Café London W1
The Vault is located in the basement of the Hard Rock Cafe shop in London. It has some incredible pieces of rock memorabilia.
Admission FREE
www.hardrock.com

Wallace Collection London W1
A national museum in an historic London town house. In 25 galleries are unsurpassed displays of French 18th century painting, furniture and porcelain, with superb Old Master paintings and a world class armoury.
Admission FREE
www.wallacecollection.org

Whitechapel Bell Foundry London E1
The museum in the foyer displays bells and a
range of Whitechapel merchandising. This is
open Monday to Friday, between 9.00am and
5.00pm.
Admission FREE
www.whitechapelbellfoundry.co.uk

Interesting Fact
Whitechapel Bell Foundry
The BIG BEN Bell is the largest bell ever made
by Whitechapel.

Section 6
More Thrifty Tips

* Remember
Our Favourite Attractions for Family visits
are marked with an asterix

Section 6
More Thrifty Tips

Art Lovers Tips

Galleries

First Thursdays
On the first Thursday of every month over 170 galleries and museums in East London are open till 9pm with free events, talks, exhibitions and private views. Each month check out the top 5 exhibitions, join the FREE Art Bus or follow one of the recommended walking tours from leading curators and writers.
www.firstthursdays.co.uk

Projects

Art in the City
Exciting sculptures from some of the world's leading artists can be found in the heart of the Square Mile. Artisits include Jake & Dinos Chapman, Antony Gormley, and Robert Indiana. For full details visit the Sculpture in the City section of the City of London website:
www.cityoflondon.gov.uk

The Big Draw
The Big Draw is the world's biggest celebration of drawing. It has grown into a month-long festival throughout October all over the UK.
www.campaignfordrawing.org/bigdraw

Royal Academy Summer Exhibition
London W1
The Summer Exhibition is an open art exhibition held annually at the Royal Academy at Burlington House, during the months of June, July, and August.
The exhibition includes paintings, prints, drawings, sculpture and it is the largest open exhibition in the UK.
www.royalacademy.org.uk

The Vauxhall Art Car Boot Fair
Brick Lane London E1
Anyone with a few quid in their pocket can become a collector for the day, and there's so much to see and do. The wonderful spirit of the Art Car Boot Fair gets a fresh injection of talent every year and all artists are hand picked. This is a unique event that no art lover should miss.
Annual Event see website for details:
Admission £5
www.artcarbootfair.com

Arts & Crafts
* Family Workshops

FREE Make and Do Events
Families with children can drop into the galleries and museums listed below for FREE Make and Do events throughout the year:

Bank of England London EC2
FREE Art & Craft activities for children during school holidays, and concert events
www.bankofengland.co.uk

Camden Arts Centre
FREE Activities
FREE Art & Craft activates for families and children.
www.camdenartscentre.org

Grant Museum of Zoology
UCL London WC1
FREE Family Fun days & Workshops
www.ucl.ac.uk/museums/zoology

Holborn Library London WC1
Autumn Art & Crafts after school in the children's library for children, carers, families.
www.camden.gov.uk

Horniman Museum London SE23
Arts & Crafts sessions
www.horniman.ac.uk

Kentish Town City Farm London NW3
Art session all these include Singsong and a cuppa parents with 0-5yrs.
Small Fee
www.ktcityfarm.org.uk

Lauderdale House
Highgate London N6
Art and music workshops for adults and children
www.lauderdalehouse.co.uk

Mudchute London City Farm
The farm has a collection of workshops available.
www.mudchute.org

National Gallery
London WC2
Free hands-on art workshops and drawing sessions every Sunday at 11am and 2pm.
www.nationalgallery.org.uk/whats-on/5-11-activities-sundays

Orleans House
FREE Arts & Crafts
FREE drop-in arts and crafts workshops for families, 2pm - 3:30pm, no booking necessary
www.richmond.gov.uk/orleans_house_gallery

Princes Drawing School
London EC2
Free Life Drawing Class
On the first Thursday of the month (6.30-9pm) there is a Free Life Drawing class.
Free Life Drawing Class
www.princesdrawingschool.org

The South London Gallery
London SE5
Free Talks & Workshops
The Gallery runs a rich and exciting
programmer of events for children and families.
Free drop-in workshops during school holidays.
www.southlondongallery.org

Somerset House
London WC2
FREE Family Workshops
www.somersethouse.org.uk

St Martins in the Field
Brass Rubbing
London W1
Brass rubbing workshops, Prices for brass
rubbing start at £4.50.
www.stmartin-in-the-fields.org

Royal Academy of Arts
FREE Workshops
FREE drop in workshops for children and
families at the RA Learning Studio - see website.
www.royalacademy.org.uk

The Topoloski Centaury
Topolski 50 plus Workshops
Open to everyone over 50 every weekday
afternoons from 2- 4pm with tea and biscuits
cost £5.
www.topolskicentury.org.uk

Art Bar

The Doodle Bar Battersea London SW11
An Art Lovers dream the Doodle Bar is designed to be a blank canvas were visitors can pop in for a drink and a scribble. Why not see if you can scribble the doodle of the month! See website for details:
www.thedoodlebar.com

Thrifty Tip
The Doodle Bar
FREE Events
The Doodle Bar also hosts FREE events
See website for details:
www.thedoodlebar.com

Design/Architecture

* Archkids Festival
Archikids Festival is Open-City's flagship architecture festival for families. In 2013, it was a three day festival aimed to excite and engage young people on the value of architecture and their city.
The weekend event allows children, and their families, time to explore the architecture of the City of London's Square Mile by participating in the festival's inspiring architectural activities, tours and workshops.
FREE Annual Event
See website
www.opencity.org.uk/education/informal/archikids.html

Heritage Open Days
National Trust
Every year buildings of every age, style and function throw open their doors. It is a chance to discover architectural treasures and enjoy a wide range of tours, events and activities that bring local history and culture to life.
FREE Annual Event
See website:
www.heritageopendays.org.uk

Open House London
FREE Event
Open House London celebrates all that is best about the capital's buildings, places and neighborhoods. Every September the FREE Open House Event gives a unique opportunity to get out and under the skin of London's amazing architecture, with over 700 buildings of all kinds opening their doors to everyone.
FREE Annual Event
See website
www.londonopenhouse.org

Bike & Boat Rides, Car Runs, Marathons & Races

Bikes

World Naked Bike Ride
London
A peaceful, imaginative and fun protest against oil dependency and car culture. A celebration of the bicycle and also a celebration of the power and individuality of the human body, and a symbol of the vulnerability of the cyclist.
FREE Annual Event
www.worldnakedbikeride.org/uk

Boats

* Clipper Round the World Race
Start & Finnish at St Katharine's Dock
St Katherine's Dock will host the start and finish of the 2013-2014 World Yacht Race. Leaving the Dock on 1 September 2013 and returning July 2014 see the website for full details:
www.skdocks.co.uk

* Great River Race
The Great River Race is London's River Marathon; it's a spectacular race up the River Thames that attracts over 300 crews from all around the world, and hundreds of spectators. The race appeals to every kind of competitor from serious athletes, to the fun competitors.
FREE Annual Event
See website
www.greatriverrace.co.uk

* Oxford and Cambridge Boat Race The Thames

The Boat Race is one of the oldest sporting events in the world. Watched by thousands along the banks of The Tideway, between Putney and Mortlake in London the Boat Race is a unique sporting event.
FREE Annual Event
See website
www.theboatrace.org

Cars

* London-Brighton Veteran Car Run Hyde Park London

This annual FREE show includes iconic vehicles to celebrate the 19th, 20th and 21st centuries of motoring.
The run can attract as many as 500 automobiles from the dawn of motoring. As the longest running motoring event in the world, it is no surprise that 500,000 onlookers turn out to enjoy a genuine and free to view spectacle.
FREE Annual Event
See website
www.veterancarrun.com

Marathons

* London Marathon

The London Marathon is a 26 mile running event that raises huge amounts of money for various charities.

Although a serious event with many elite runners taking part there is also a great fun side to the race with many participants dressing up. Thousands line the streets to cheer on the runners every year and watching the race is really a fun day out.

FREE Annual Event
See website
www.virginlondonmarathon.com

Carnivals Festivals & Parades

Carnivals

* Notting Hill Carnival
London W11

Held each August Bank Holiday since 1966, the Notting Hill Carnival is the largest festival celebration of its kind in Europe. Every year the streets of West London come alive with the sounds and smells of Europe's biggest street festival. Sunday is traditionally Children's day, and Monday is Adults day.

FREE Annual Event
August Bank Holiday Weekend
See website:
www.thenottinghillcarnival.com

Thrifty Tip
Notting Hill

Notting Hill is one of London's trendiest areas with flea markets, markets, and shops full of vintage fashion and antiques it's a must visit for any fashionista, or antique lover.

Festivals

* Angel Canal Festival London N1

This annual one-day festival held in September is based around the City Road Lock, Basin and towpath alongside the Regents Canal, also local streets and a park, in Islington.

Attractions include Stalls, a Children's Fun Fair with Rides & Bouncy Castles, Punch & Judy, Story-teller, Boat Trips, Art Projects including free have a go pottery sessions.

With an outdoor Art Gallery, Live Music (Folk, Ska, Brass, Jazz, Ukuleles) & Street Theatre.

There is also a Regatta with free have a go canoeing sessions and Bell-Boat Racing.

FREE Annual Event

See website

www.angelcanalfestival.org

* Canal Cavalcade
Little Venice London W9

The annual canal festival in Little Venice orgainised by the Inland Waterways Association since the 1980s and is very popular. Attractions include Stalls, and Children's Fun Fair.

The highlight of the weekend is the Sunday night illuminated boat procession followed by live music.

FREE Annual Event

See website

www.canalandrivercruises.com/canalway-cavalcade

* City of London Festival

The Festival exists to entertain and inspire the City's workers, residents and visitors with

special events and world-class artists in beautiful surroundings.
FREE Annual Event
See website
www.colf.org

* Greenwich
FREE International Festival
Don't miss the Annual FREE Greenwich International Festival. With a line up of International and UK Outdoor Arts, including outdoor theatre, outdoor dance, and installations.
See website for dates:
www.ornc.org/events/detail/greenwichdoc klands-international-festival1

* London Design Festival
The London Design Festival is held to celebrate and promote London as the design capital of the World.
FREE Annual Event
See website
www.londondesignfestival.com

* New Cross and Deptford
FREE Film Festval
Events include film screenings, filmmaking, children's films, and discussions.
FREE Annual Event
See website
www.freefilmfestivals.org

*** Punch & Judy Puppet Festival
& May Fayre FREE Event
St Paul's Church London WC2**
The Puppet Festival & May Fayre take place in the garden of St Paul's Church. The day starts with a Grand Procession led by the Superior Brass Band, followed by the Special Church Service at 12noon, and performances until 5.30pm.
**FREE Annual Event
See website
www.punchandjudy.com**

**Interesting Fact
Puppet Festival Mr Punch**
Samuel Pepys first saw the puppet Mr Punch in Covent Garden in May 1662, it was recorded in his diary.

* Regent Street Festival London W1
This annual event sees Regent Street pedestrianised for the day. The theme for the festival in 2013 was 'Fashion'. There was catwalk shows in the street and makeovers in the stores as well as lots of special offers and live music.
**FREE Annual Event
See website
www.regentstreetonline.com**

*** Southbank Centre
Summer Festival London SE1**
The Southbank centre hold Annual Summer Festivals with different themes.

For Summer 2013 they asked artists, designers, architects and community groups to help turn the Southbank Centre into London's friendliest neighbourhood.

Visitors can join in with activities, watch events and explore the colourful, imaginative free installations around the site.

FREE Annual Event
See website
www.southbankcentre.co.uk

Interesting Fact
Southbank Summer Festival 2013
The 2013 Festival saw a beach and beach huts brought to the Southbank.

* Thrifty Tip
Southbank Centre
Fountain
Jeppe Hein's "Appearing Rooms" fountain is outside Queen Elizabeth Hall Southbank Centre. The fountain is great fun for children of all ages, and a fantastic fun way to cool off on a hot summers day.

* The Thames Festival London
Thousands of people turn out for the Thames Festival it brings the summer to a close in spectacular style. There is singing and dancing, amazing performances, great food, and great fun atmosphere.

FREE Annual Event
See website
www.thamesfestival.org

* The Twelfth Night Festival
Bankside London
An annual seasonal celebration held in bankside.
It is a celebration of the New Year, mixing
ancient seasonal customs with contemporary
festivity, it includes Music Dance and Theatre
see website for full details:
FREE Annual Event
See website
www.thelionspart.co.uk/twelfthnight

Festivals Literature

* London Literature Festival
Southbank London SE1
The Southbank Centre's annual London
Literature Festival includes Best-selling authors
reading from and discussing their work. There is
also live poetry, short plays, music and
discussions.
FREE Annual Event
See website:
www.londonlitfest.com

* Thrifty Tip
Children's Literature
Horniman Museum
During AUG/SEPT their popular storytellers
bring their collections and gardens alive with
enchanting stories from around the world.
See the website for details:
www.horniman.ac.uk

Thrifty Tip for Book Lovers

Daunt Bookshop
Hampstead London NW3
Free walking book group meets every last
Sunday of the month at 11.30 on Hampstead
Heath.
www.dauntbooks.co.uk

Parades

* Harrods Santa Parade
London SW1
The parade is led by Father Christmas and
accompanied by giant teddy bears, street
dancers and real-life reindeer.
Annual Event
See website:
www.harrods.com

Interesting Fact
Harrods
Diana Princess of Wales &
Dodi Al-Fayed Memorials
Since the deaths of Diana Princess of Wales,
and Dodi Al-Fayed two memorials to the
couple have been erected inside Harrods.

* Lord Mayors Parade and Show
London
The Lord Mayor's Show has been a part of
almost 800 years of London history it survived
the Black Death and the blitz. It is one of the
21st century's best loved pageants with floats,
marching bands, music and much more.

The show ends with an amazing Firework Display.
FREE Annual Event
See website:
www.lordmayorsshow.org/

Parades/New Year Celebrations

* Chinese New Year London W1
London hosts the biggest Chinese New Year Celebrations outside of China at Trafalgar Square and China Town. The celebrations include live shows by Chinese performers and dancers. Central London comes alive with Chinese culture in a celebration marking the beginning of a new year.
FREE Annual Event
See website:
www.chinatownlondon.org

* New Year's Day Parade
London W1
London's New Year's Day Parade is the World's Largest New Year's Day Parade. Performers from all over the world participate in the parade and highlights include marching bands, cheerleaders, clowns, acrobats, kites and much more. Large crowds attend the event which befits the historic 2.2 mile route from The Ritz Hotel in Piccadilly to Parliament Sq.
FREE Annual Event
See website:
www.londonparade.co.uk

Royal Parades

* Trooping the Colour London

The Sovereign's official birthday is celebrated by the ceremony of Trooping the Colour on a Saturday in June. The parade is carried out by operational troops. There are marching bands and horses, and it is a true spectacle of English Pageantry.

The parade is attended by the Queen and other members of the Royal family. The parade ends with The Queen and membersof the Royal family on the balcony at Buckingham Palace and an RAF fly past.

FREE Annual Event
See website:
www.royal.gov.uk

Ceremonies

Ceremony of the Keys
Tower of London EC3

The Ceremony of the Keys is the traditional locking up of the Tower of London. It has taken place each night, without fail, for at least 700 years.

Ceremony Admission FREE
Apply in writing see website.
www.hrp.org.uk

Interesting Fact
Ceremony of the Keys

The importance of securing thefortress for the night is still very relevant because, although the Monarch no longer resides at this royal palace, the Crown Jewels and many other valuables still do.

Changing the Guard

* Buckingham Palace London SW1
At Buckingham Palace Changing the Guard takes place at 11.30am. The Foot Guards provide a colourful display in their red tunics and bearskins and are accompanied by a band throughout. It is held daily from May to July, and on alternate dates throughout the rest of the year see website:
www.royal.gov.uk/RoyalEventsandCeremonies

Interesting Fact
Buckingham Palace
When the Royal Standard flag flies on the roof of Buckingham Palace the Queen is in residence.

Interesting Fact
The Queen
The Queen was born on 21 April 1926, her birthplace was 17 Bruton Street London W1.

The young princess Elizabeth was the first child of The Duke and Duchess of York, who later became King George VI and Queen Elizabeth.

* Horse Guards Arch London W1
At Horse Guards Arch, Changing the Guard takes place daily at 11.00am (10.00 am on Sundays) and lasts about half an hour; it is normally held on Horse Guards Parade by the arch of Horse Guards Building see website: **www.royal.gov.uk/RoyalEventsandCeremonies**

English Heritage

English Heritage
Blue Plaques Scheme
London's blue plaques scheme commemorates the link between notable figures of the past and the buildings in which they lived and worked. The properties are FREE to view from the outside below is a small selection of the figures whos properties are available to view:

Jane Austen Author, Isambard Kingdom Brunel Civil Engineer, Charles Darwin, Charles Dickens, John Logie Baird inventor, Constable Artist/Painter, Karl Marx, Mozart, Sir Isaac Newton, Napoleon 111, George Orwell Author, Samuel Pepys Diarist, Shelley and many more. To find an address of where a notable figure of the past lived or worked visit the English Heritage website: **www.english-heritage.org.uk/discover/blue-plaques/search**

Interesting Fact
Charles Dickens &
The George and the Vulture
London EC3
Charles Dickens drank at The George and The Vulture pub, and it is mentioned at least 20 times in *The Pickwick Papers.*

Entertainment

Ballet Opera & Film Screenings

Ballet & Opera Screenings

BP Outdoor FREE Screenings
Trafalgar Square London WC2
At the outdoor screenings you can enjoy world class Opera and Ballet in true alfresco style with the summer FREE live relays from the Royal Opera House. Venues include Trafalgar Square & Victoria Park.
For summer listings see website:
www.roh.org.uk/about/bp-big-screens

Film Screenings

Bea's Tea Room
Bloomsbury
Movie Nights
Events at Bea's include Movie nights from as little as £5 see website:
www.beasofbloomsbury.com/events

Goeth Institute
FREE Screenings
London SW7
FREE Events throughout the year including
film screenings
www.goethe.de/ins/gb/lon

* New Cross & Deptford
FREE Film Festival
Events include film screenings, filmmaking,
children's films, and discussions.
www.freefilmfestivals.org

* The Scoop Amphitheatre
London SE1
FREE Screenings & Theatre
This sunken space seats 800 and can be found
beside City Hall, close to Tower Bridge. During
summer months the amphitheatre hosts many
FREE events including live music, plays, film
screenings and classes.
www.morelondon.com/scoop.html

White Cube Bermondsey
London SE1
FREE Film Screenings
White Cube has several FREE events including
FREE Sunday Film Screenings see website for
listings:
www.whitecube.com

Other Screenings

* Canary Wharf Canada Square Park
FREE Summer-Screens London
Enjoy a packed programme of sports and
entertainment in Canada Square Park on the
Summer Screens.
Highlights include Wimbledon and other
sporting events. Fascinating archive footage of
London, highlights from the Proms at the Royal
Albert Hall plus news and current affairs from
BBC News24 and entertainment from all the
BBC channels.
Annual summer event see website for dates:
www.canarywharf.com

Entertainment/Music
Blues, Jazz & Folk

National Theatre
Djanogly Concert Pitch in the Foyer
The concert pitch offers Jazz & Folk music
Mon-Fri 5.45 Sat 1pm, and occasional Sundays.
Admission FREE
www.nationaltheatre.org.uk

National Portrait Gallery London WC2
Late Shift in partnership with FTI Consulting
offers new ways to explore the Gallery after
hours and socialise after work.
Enjoy a wide range of events including
FREE live music every Friday from 6.30pm
www.npg.org.uk

Royal Festivl Hall SE1
Central Bar
London SE1
Royal Festival Hall has a wealth of free workshops that take place in the main bar, there is always something interesting going on to catch your attention. Friday FREE lunchtimes music.
See website for details:
FREE Music
www.southbankcentre.co.uk

*** The Scoop Amphitheatre**
London South Bank
London SE1
This sunken space seats 800 and can be found beside City Hall, close to Tower Bridge. During summer months, the amphitheatre is in use almost every evening, hosting live music, plays, and film screenings.
FREE
www.morelondon.com/scoop.html

St Pancras Railway Station
London N1
The Station Sessions in St Pancras International showcase the best new music FREE every Thursday from 5:30pm to 6:30pm. Find them in their new upstairs location on the Grand Terrace.
FREE
www.stpancras.com/station-sessions

**Southbank Centre
London SE1**
Regularly hosts FREE live music on Friday evenings from leading musicians performing everything from jazz and blues to folk. Alternatively drop in for free lunchtime music in the Central Bar of the Royal Festival Hall on Fridays and Sundays.
Admission FREE
www.southbankcentre.co.uk

Wiltons Music Hall London E1
Wiltons Mahogany Bar introduces a FREE night of toe tapping, drawing on the crème de la crème of London's Jazz talent. From 4th September join them every Tuesday for a night of classic swing music from the 20s, 30s and 40s performed live by The London Dance Orchestra. See website for full listings.
Admission FREE
www.wiltons.org.uk

Entertainment Music
Jazz Festivals London

London Jazz Festival Southbank
The London Jazz Festival, produced by Serious in association with BBC Radio 3, is the capital's biggest pan-city music festival. The Festival has long been acclaimed for showcasing a heady mix of talent from around the world. Widely acknowledged for delivering world-class artists and emerging stars, one of UK's landmark music events.
Many FREE Events
www.southbankcentre.co.uk

Entertainment Music Pop & Rock

Dublin Castle Camden London NW1

The Dublin Castle is a legendary pub and music venue. The Dublin Castle stage has been graced by everyone from Blur, through Coldplay, Madness, Supergrass, The Killers, The Arctic Monkeys, and Billy Bragg. Features 4 live bands every night.
FREE
www.thedublincastle.com

Forge & Foundry Camden NW1

The Forge Venue has been specially designed by the award-winning Burd Haward Architects. With natural acoustics it's Ideal for musical performances.
Admission FREE Some Nights
Seee website:
www.foundrycamden.co.uk

* Thrifty Tip
Camden Lock

Camden Lock is one of London's trendiest areas. As well as a great number of FREE music venues, its full of stalls and shops with plenty of vintage home ware and fashion, it's a must visit for any vintage lover.
With food from around the world the Lock is also a great place to sit and eat or just sit and watch the world go by.
www.camdenlockmarket.com

Entertainment Music/ Concerts & Recitals

City Music Society City London EC2
The City Music Society will be running a series of weekly **FREE** Winter Concerts from January 2013.
Check the website for more information.
FREE
www.citymusicsociety.org/Free.htm

Christ Church Spitalfields E1
FREE Concerts and Recitals take place at the Church see website.
http://ccspitalfields.org/welcome

Imperial College
South Kensington & Hammersmith SW7
The lunchtime concert series is one of the jewels in Imperial's crown with world-class performers. Concerts take place at 1 pm every Thursday during term time on the South Kensington campus, and regularly on Tuesdays on the Hammersmith campus.
Admission FREE
www.3.imperial.ac.uk/arts/music

Royal College of Music
London SW7
FREE lunchtime recitals at various locations throughout London.
See their website for full listings:
www.rcm.ac.uk

St Margaret's Church
London SW1
FREE Recitals & Carol Services
Recitles during the summer, and they also have
FREE Carol Services in December for full
listings see the website:
www.Westminster-abbey.org/st-margarets

St Martins in the Fields
London WC2
St Martin-in-the-Fields is a busy working church
with over 20 services and 6-7concerts per week.
FREE Lunchtime Concerts
www.smitf.org

St Mary Le Bow Church
London EC2
FREE Live Chamber Music
FREE Organ Recitals
Concerts take place at 1.05pm daily. They also
hold FREE Organ Recitals.
See website for listings.
www.stmarylebow.co.uk

St Paul's Cathedral
London EC4
FREE Sunday Organ Recitals
Sunday Organ Recitals take place weekly at
4.45pm. These recitals are free and last about 30
minutes.
All are welcome to attend.
See website:
www.stpauls.co.uk

* Spitalfields London E1
FREE Events
Spitalfields, winner of the 2007 Best New Open Space offers FREE events including lunchtime concerts and more visit website for the full listings:
www.spitalfields.co.uk

Wesleys Chapel
London EC1
Wesley's Chapels FREE recitals are a staple of city life, showcasing talented musicians and a variety of music.
FREE lunchtime recitals on Tuesdays
www.wesleyschapel.org.uk

Entertainment Music Opera

Holland Park Opera
London W11
The OHP Inspire Project aims to inspire and encourage all members of the community to experience classical music.
As part of this project in 2012 OHP gave away five hundred FREE tickets to encourage both opera novices and the more experienced to try a new repertoire. To see what is on offer now visit the website:
www.operahollandpark.com

Entertainment Music Other

* Canary Wharf
London E14

Enjoy live music from emerging artists on the summer stage as a variety of artists provide the perfect musical accompaniment to enjoying your lunch alfresco style in Canada Square Park.
www.canarywharf.com

Horniman Museum Gardens

The Horniman Gardens have a weekly series of bandstand concerts, see website for listings:
www.horniman.ac.uk

National Sound Archive
British Library

The British Library Sounds website provides free online access for UK higher and further education institutions.

With over 50,000 rare recordings of music, spoken word, and human and natural environments. Many of these recordings are also accessible for general public listening online.
http://sounds.bl.uk

Royal Academy of Music Museum
London NW1

The museum regularly hosts exhibitions and events including daily live demonstrations on their historic pianos.

They welcome all members of the public, students and families.

Admission FREE

www.ram.ac.uk/museum

* Royal Albert Hall
The Proms £5 Tickets
London SW7

The BBC Proms at The RAH has the popular tradition of Promming (standing in the Arena or Gallery areas of the RAH) it is central to the unique atmosphere. Up to 1,400 Standing places are available for each Proms concert. The traditionally low prices allow you to enjoy world-class performances.

Promming places are available on the door £5.00 each.

www.royalalberthall.com

* The Scoop Amphitheatre
South Bank London SE1

This sunken space seats 800 and can be found beside City Hall, close to Tower Bridge.

During summer months the amphitheatre is in use almost every evening, hosting live music, plays, film screenings and classes many of which are FREE.

For FREE listings see website:
www.morelondon.com/scoop.html

* The Queen Elizabeth Hall

Queen Elizabeth Hall hosts chamber orchestras, quartets, choirs, dance performances and opera.

As well as the main concert hall the Queen Elizabeth Hall also contains two smaller venues, the Purcell Room and The Front Room at the QEH.
For FREE listings see the website:
www.southbankcentre.co.uk

Thrifty Tip
Handel House Museum London W1
Handel House Museum invites musicians wanting to rehearse repertoire from the baroque period to apply to use the Rehearsal and Performance Room.
www.handelhouse.org

Entertainment Street Performances

* Broadgate London
Broadgate has a piano situated just off Finsbury Avenue Square by Costa Coffee. Play away in a quiet and private area of Broadgate Monday to Sunday between 07:00hrs to 19:00.
FREE
www.broadgate.co.uk

* Brick Lane
London E1
Brick Lane market on Sundays has an array of street performers to enhance the vibrant, lively atmosphere.
FREE
www.visitbricklane.org

Interesting Facts
Brick Lane E1
Brick Lane is very popular with London's young and trendy crowd, with its mix of vintage shops and street art it's a fascinating and exciting place to visit.

Brick Lane is also the Curry Capital of the UK, it has many many authentic curry houses.

* Covent Garden London WC1
The Street Performers of Covent Garden are all auditioned acts and they perform finely crafted shows. Downstairs in the market hall you can see the most amazing Opera singers completely FREE, including Sergio Barros (who you can view on Youtube).
FREE
www.coventgardenlondonuk.com

* Spitalfields London E1
Spitalfields, winner of the 2007 Best New Open Space also offers **FREE** events including lunchtime concerts, festivals, tango classes, fashion shows and much more.
See website for the full listings:
www.spitalfields.co.uk

* Southbank London SE1
Many street performers line the street along the side of the Thames at the Southbank. The South Bank centre also has many free performances and events throughout the year.
FREE See website for listings:
www.southbankcentre.co.uk

Entertainment Theatre

* FREE Theatre Tickets for Under 26's
The Arts Council developed the A Night Less Ordinary scheme in association with Metro. The scheme offers over half a million FREE Theatre Tickets to anyone under 26 at more than 200 venues.
www.artscouncil.org.uk

Arcola Theatre Hackney
London E8
The Arcola Theatre sets aside a certain number of tickets for their "Pay What You Can" Night on Tuesdays see website:
www.arcolatheatre.com

* Canary Wharf Outdoor Theatre
London E14
Enjoy a summer celebration at Canary Wharf of free outdoor family theatre with performances especially designed for children and adults to enjoy together.
See Events section of the website:
FREE
www.canarywharf.com

* Kid's week (5-16 year olds)
Society of London Theatre
Kids Week is all about introducing young people to the magic of theatre. A child 16 or under can go free to a participating show when with an adult at certain times during the summer, see website:
www.kidsweek.co.uk

* October Plenty Southwark
Autumn harvest celebration held in Southwark.
Beginning on Bankside by Shakespeare's Globe.
October plenty mixes ancient seasonal customs
and theatre with modern festivity, joining in
with the historic Borough Market's Apple Day
celebrations.
FREE Annual Event
See website:
www.boroughmarket.org.uk

Royal Opera House London WC2
Standing Tickets £6
The Royal Opera House stages performances
from both The Royal Ballet and The Royal
Opera.
Many of the world's finest performers from
these fields have performed here including
Dame Margot Fonteyn and Rudolf Nureyev
(Ballet) and Plácido Domingo, Luciano
Pavarotti and Joan Sutherland (Opera).
Standing tickets at the ROH start from as little
as £6.
www.roh.org.uk

Thrifty Tip
Royal Opera House
BP Outdoor Screenings
Trafalgar Square & Victoria Park
At the outdoor screenings you can enjoy world
class Opera and Ballet in true alfresco style with
the summer FREE live relays from the Royal
Opera House. Venues include Trafalgar Square
& Victoria Park.
For listings see website:
www.roh.org.uk/about/bp-big-screens

Royal Opera House Cinema

ROH Cinema is another way to see Ballet & Opera at reduced prices see ROH website for Cinema listings:
www.roh.org.uk/about/cinema

* The Scoop Amphitheatre
London SE1

This sunken space seats 800 and can be found beside City Hall close to Tower Bridge. During summer months the amphitheatre is in use almost every evening, hosting live theatre, music and film screenings classes.
FREE Events see website for listings:
www.morelondon.com/scoop.html

Shakespeare's Globe Theatre
Bankside London SE1
Yardstanding Tickets Only £5

Shakespeare's Globe is a unique international resource dedicated to the exploration of Shakespeare's work. There are 700 £5 yard standing tickets for every performance. Yard Standing offers the best view of the stage, and is an amazing experience.
www.shakespearesglobe.com

St Brides Foundation
London EC4

St Brides Foundation has a lunchbox Theatre where you can watch a performance from as little as £6.
See website for listings:
www.sbf.org.uk

* Twelfth Night
Bankside London
An annual seasonal celebration held in bankside.
It is a celebration of the New Year, mixing
ancient seasonal customs with contemporary
festivity; it includes Theatre, Music and Dance
see website for full details:
FREE Annual Event
www.thelionspart.co.uk/twelfthnight

* West End Live
Trafalgar Square
London WC1
West End LIVE is an annual London event that
showcases the quality and diversity of
entertainment on offer in the heart of London,
promoting the West End as an exciting venue
for all the family.
All live and all for free in the iconic setting of
Trafalgar Square.
FREE Annual Event
See website:
www.westendlive.co.uk

Theatre Get Involved

* Roundhouse Theatre
Take Part
London NW1
If you're 11 to 25 years old and like being
creative, you'll find something to capture your
imagination at the Roundhouse take part,
including radio and music production, drama,
poetry, TV, sound engineering, photography
and visual arts, see website:
www.roundhouse.org.uk/take-part

* Thrifty Tip
Roundhouse
iTunes Festival
FREE Gig
The iTunes Festival is 30 nights of free gigs held at the Roundhouse. Previous performers have included: Justin Timberlake, and Jessie J. For full details of dates and how to appy for tickets see website:
www.roundhouse.org.uk

Entertainment/ TV Studio Shows

* BFI Mediatech South Bank
London SE1
This suite of wide-screen computer booths offers FREE access to thousands of archive TV shows, films and documentaries. Also film screening from as little as £5.
See website for listings:
www.bfi.org.uk

BBC
FREE Tickets
The BBC aims to involve all sections of their audience in making shows. They want to encourage people of all ages, backgrounds and abilities to apply to participate as members of studio audiences and contributors to programmes, to tour their buildings and to join at events.
To apply for FREE tickets to shows visit:
www.bbc.co.uk/showsandtours/tickets/

ITV
FREE Tickets
Would you like to be part of the studio audience watching your favourite ITV show? Applause Store is a one-stop-shop offering free tickets to lots of ITV shows including The X Factor, Britain's Got Talent.
To apply for FREE tickets to shows visit:
www.applausestore.com/home.ph

Exhibitions

London's Art Galleries and Museums have an ever changing program of exhibitions and events; see the individual Galleries/Museum websites for details most of these are
Admission FREE

Royal Opera House Exhibitions
London WC2
Royal Opera House Collections manages a constantly changing programme of exhibitions. Each season, between September and August, there are two main Exhibitions that fill the costume cases and the Amphitheatre Gallery for approximately four consecutive months.
A series of smaller Spotlight Exhibitions fill some of the wall cases and foyer areas for periods of four to six weeks through the season.
Admission FREE to Exhibitions
See website:
www.roh.org.uk/visit/exhibitions

Fashion Hair & Beauty

Charity Shops
Shopping in charity shops is a thrifty way to purchase vintage on a budget, and London has some real gems. A few of our favourites are listed below to find a charity shop close to you visit the Charity Retail Association website: **www.charityretail.org.uk**

British Red Cross
Old Church Street Chelsea
London SW3
This expansive store is arguably Chelsea's most popular, well-known and well-loved charity shop - packed with vintage.
www.redcross.org.uk

Oxfam Shop
Camden High Street
London NW1
Great for vintage finds, you will need to have good rummage through.
There are some very good bargains to be had. **Tel: 0207 387 4354**
www.oxfam.org.uk

Oxfam Boutique
Westbourne Grove London W11
Great for vintage finds very popular with fashionister's and models.
Tel: 0207 229 5000

Fashion/
London's Trendy Markets

London's trendy markets are also a great place to pick up preloved or vintage bargains. Below is a list of our favourites:

* Brick Lane
London E1
Brick Lane market great for vintage clothing and accessories, you may need to have a good rummage.
See website:
www.visitbricklane.org

Camden Lock
London NW1
Camden Lock is one of London's trendiest areas. There is plenty of vintage home ware and fashion, it's a must visit for any vintage lover.
See website:
www.camdenlockmarket.com

Portobello Road
Notting Hill
London
Portobello Road Notting Hill is one of London's trendiest areas with flea markets, markets, and shops full of vintage fashion and antiques it's a must visit for any fashionista, vintage or antique lover.
See Website:
www.portobelloroad.co.uk

Hair

London Beauty Institute
London WC2
FREE Haircuts
At LBI they know that if you look good, you feel good. Why not book yourself in for a fabulous new look.
FREE haircuts on offer from students
www.londonbeautyinstitute.com/FreeTreatments.htm

L'Oreal Hammersmith
London W6
FREE Haircuts and Colouring
Top hair care brand L'Oreal is always looking for hair models for both cutting and colouring first appointment FREE.
FREE Haircuts and Colouring from students
www.loreal.co.uk

Saks Academies
Covent Garden
London WC2
Saks always require Models for Hair and Beauty Training Sessions haircuts from £5. They also have Beauty services ranging from Manicures and Tanning to Indian Head and Aromatherapy Massages.
www.sakstraining1.rtrk.co.uk

Beauty

London Beauty Institute
Covent Garden
London WC2
FREE Beauty Treatments
At LBI they know that if you look good, you feel good.
Why not book yourself in for one of the many fabulous FREE beauty treatments from eye lash extensions to facials.
FREE Beauty Treatments from students
www.londonbeautyinstitute.com/FreeTreatments.htm

London College of Beauty Therapy
London W1
The college offers low rate treatments carried out by students trained in the latest industry techniques. Take a look at the website for treatments on offer and be amazed at how little they cost, many for £5 or less.
www.lcbt.co.uk/lcbtsalon

Ulamasqua School of Makeup
Beak Street London W1
FREE Beauty Treatments
FREE Drop in Beauty at Ulamasque School of make up in Beak Street London.
www.illamasqua.com

Saks Academies
Covent Garden London WC2
Offer a wide range of Beauty treatments services ranging from Manicures and Tanning

to Indian Head and Aromatheraphy Massages.
Waxing from £5
www.saks.co.uk

Food & Drink

Afternoon Tea

Afternoon tea a quintessentially English practice
was introduced by the seventh Duchess of
Bedford in 1840. Afternoon Tea can be
expensive in London however check out
Groupon as you can often find Afternoon Tea
available at very Thrifty prices.
www.groupon.co.uk

Cream Tea

Cream tea (usually includes scones clotted
cream and tea) is another quintessentially
English practice and is a lot cheaper than
Afternoon Tea. Below are our favourite &
most thrifty Cream Teas – Enjoy!

Bea's Tea Room
St Pauls & Bloomsbury

A beautiful tea room with amazing pastry chefs
www.beasofbloomsbury.com

* Bea's Tea Room Events

Events include Movie Nights from £5

* Camellias Tea House Soho
London W1
This quirky tea rooms is on the top floor of
Kingly Court, off Carnaby Street.
Cream Teas which include scones, strawberry
jam and clotted cream and a choice of different
pots of tea from only £6.50
www.camelliasteahouse.com

* Crusting Pipe
Covent Garden Courtyard
Amazing setting the crusting pipe has an
outdoor courtyard, often with live Operatic
performances; you take tea you can listen to the
Opera - beautiful!
Tea with cake from £7
www.crustingpipe.co.uk

* Drink Shop Do Kings Cross
Tea and yummy cake, in very creative
surroundings.
www.drinkshopdo.com

FREE Events
Drink Shop Do
Drink Shop Do offer many FREE craft events.
Sundays there is FREE scrabble. Also FREE
music nights on Friday and Saturday.
See website:
www.drinkshopdo.com

* Fan Museum Greenwich
Afternoon Tea
Afternoon Tea is served Tuesdays and Sundays
in the Museums beautiful orangery.

Afternoon Tea is £6 per person and includes Tea/Coffee, Scnes Cream and Jam, and Homemade Cakes – Booking recommended.
www.thefanmuseum.org.uk

Interesting Fact
Fan Museum
The Orangery s decorated with a beautiful mural by Jane Barraclough which gives the room a wonderful atmosphere, and it overlooks a 'secret' garden in the Japanese manner, with a fan shaped parterre, pond, stream and oriental architectural features.

Liberty Store
London W1
This mock Tudor store is a beautiful store and one of the last great emporiums for innovative design. Situated in the heart of London since 1875, it remains to this day the destination of choice for the savvy and sophisticated shopper - don't miss the amazing window displays.
Café Liberty offers a pot of tea with a trio of parties for only £6.45.
www.liberty.co.uk

Interesting Fact
Liberty
Oscar Wilde said *"Liberty is the chosen resort of the artistic shopper."*

Soho Secret Tea Rooms
London W1
Situated above the Coach& Horses pub in Soho you will find the Soho Secret Tea Rooms,.

A shabby chic style tea rooms with vintage table cloths and china, where 40s Jazz & Swing Music plays on a gramaphone. Cream Tea is £7.50 and consists two delicious freshly baked scones cream and homemade jam, and a pot of tea.
www.sohossecrettearoom.co.uk

* Tate Modern Art Gallery
London SE1

The Tate Modern is an institution that houses International Modern and Contemporary Art. The permanent collection includes work by Miro, Monet, Picasso, Jackson Pollock and more.

With great views of London the café at Tate Modern is a great place to take tea, Pot of Tea for two with two scones with clotted cream and jam £5.50.
www.tate.org.uk/visit/tate-modern

* Victoria & Albert Museum London SW7

The world's greatest museum of art and design has a beautiful tiled café where they serve a large scone & pot of tea for one for only £6
www.vam.ac.uk

Tea Tasting

Teanamu Chaya Teahouse W11
FREE Tea Tasting

A marvellous oasis of peace and tranquillity close by bustling Portobello Road. Teanamu offer free tea tasting sessions.
See website for full details:
www.teanamu.com/teahouse

Teanamu Chaya Teahouse
Live Art FREE Events
The live art events include musicians, poets, painters, sculptors, performance artists, anyone with a message to convey or a talent to share. See website for details:

Twinning's Museum London WC2
A small museum where you can see some fascinating stuff including old teapots and caddies and some lovely old pictures of the Twining family.
FREE Tea tasting available see website:
http://shop.twinings.co.uk/shop/Strand

Food Demonstrations/ Food Sampling

* Borough Market
Demonstration Kitchen
London SE1
If you love cooking don't miss Borough Markets Demonstration Kitchen see website to see what they are cooking up next:
www.boroughmarket.org.uk

* Borough Market
Apple Day
London SE1
Autumn harvest celebration held in Borough Market. This family celebration of the seasonal apple harvest offers visitors the opportunity to sample apple varieties and products.

These include limited edition Apple Day
preserves, pies and juices.
FREE Annual Event
See website for details:
www.boroughmarket.org.uk

Calthorpe Community
FREE Cooking & Growing
Holiday, after-school and weekend programmes
provide outdoor, creative and social activities
Free Cooking, Growing activities.
See website for full details:
Admission FREE
www.calthorpeproject.org.uk

* Spitalfields City Farm London E1
Pick & Grow Sessions
FREE **Pick and Cook Sessions** are an
opportunity to learn how to cook using garden
produce to create tasty, interesting and
nutritious meals, and to share food in a friendly
setting.
See website for details:
Admission FREE
www.spitalfieldscityfarm.org

Thrifty Tip Food

If you love all things food don't forget to visit
Fortnum & Mason (it has held a Royal warrant
for over 150 years), Harrods and Selfridges
Food Halls.

Food & Drink/Water

Drinking Fountains FREE

London has many drinking fountains available (don't pay for expensive bottled water) to find a drinking fountain near you visit The Drinking Fountain Association website:
www.drinkingfountains.org

Food Lunch/Dinner

Bistro 1 London W1

For a thrifty meal we love Bistro 1 Mediterranean restaurant in either Covent Garden or Soho. Here you can have a two course meal for £8.50 and a three course meal for £9.90 great value and very good food.
www.bistro1.co.uk

Rock and Sole Plaice
Covent Garden London WC2

London's oldest Fish & Chip shop selling yummy inexpensive Fish Chips and more.
www.rockandsoleplaice.com

Gifts

Harrods London SW1

Harrods is a great place to buy tasteful inexpensive gifts from trinkets to small food gifts there really is an amazing choice many at under £5.
www.harrods.com

Fortnum & Mason London W1
Fortnum & Mason (held a Royal warrant
for over 150 years). This store is a great place to
buy inexpensive food gifts.

Health & Fitness

Gyms

FREE Outdoor Gym Company
The Great Outdoor Gym Company has joined
together with local councils to provide FREE
outdoor gyms across the country.

To find a FREE outdoor Gym close to you just
visit the website and enter your postcode:
www.tgogc.com

Meditation

Inner Space
Covent Garden London WC2
At Inner Space in Covent Garden discover
shelves of inspiring books, cds and lots more.
You can also pop into the Quiet Room, an oasis
of calm, where you can chill or simply meditate.
FREE
www.innerspace.org.uk

Running Clubs

London Running Club
FREE TRIAL
Contact Run Club London and try their
London Running Club for FREE.

Experience the premier London running club. To book a free session with a professional coaches visit the website:
www.runclub.co.uk

Nike Town London
FREE Running Club

Nike Town RC provides runners with a free and safe twice-weekly training hub. Held every Monday (ladies night) and Tuesday (males/females), membership is FREE and runners of all abilities are welcome to join.

All runs are led and supervised by Nike staff and runners are advised to arrive at Nike Town at 6pm to allow plenty of time to stretch before setting off. Refreshments are provided upon return to Nike Town London.
Tel: 0207 612 0800

Park Run
FREE WEEKLY

Park Run organise free weekly 5km timed runs in London. They are open to everyone FREE and are safe and easy to take part in. These events take place in pleasant parkland surroundings and are designed for people of all ability to take part; from those taking their first steps in running to Olympians from juniors to those with more experience.

Every Saturday 9am London Parks include Hampstead Heath, Highbury Fields, Dulwich Park and more.
See website for a park near you.
www.parkrun.org.uk/home

Swimming

* London Lidos
London has many Lidos (open air swimming pools) a great way to cool down on a beautiful summer's day. Many of the Lidos date back to the 30's and are in the beautiful Art Deco style. Swimming at the Lido's is very inexpensive and some offer Free swimming for disabled people and their carers under 18s and over 60s.
See individual websites below:

Central London

Oasis Sports Centre London WC2
www.camden.gov.uk

Serpentine Lido London W2
www.royalparks.org.uk

East London

London Fields Lido London E8
The capital's only Olympic-size heated outdoor pool.
www.hackney.gov.uk/c-londonfields-lido.htm

North London

Finchley Lido London N12
www.barnet.gov.uk

Park Road Leicure Centre London N8
www.haringey.gov.uk

Parliament Hill London NW5
www.camden.gov.uk

Other Lido's

Richmond Pool Richmond Park
www.springhealth.net/richmond

Swimming Ponds

Hampstead Heath Ponds
Open-air swimming is internationally famous on
Hampstead Heath with the Ladies' Pond, the
Men's Pond, the Mixed Pond.

The Ladies' and Men's Ponds are unique in the
U K in being the only life-guarded open-water
swimming facilities open to the public every day
of the year.
Tel: 020 7485 3873
www.cityoflondon.gov.uk

Outdoor Swimming Society
As well as the free social swims that go on all
year round the Outdoor Swimming Society
holds a few big events every year.
www.outdoorswimmingsociety.com

Table Tennis

* Table Tennis (Play Ping Pong)
FREE

Ping is an innovative street ping pong project which provides people with opportunities to play social and competitive table tennis, free of charge. The aim is to get as many people as possible across the whole of the UK playing. Ping sees a month of activity and tables popping up in unusual and remarkable places. Marked 'Stop and Play', the tables are for all to enjoy to join in the fun is website:
www.pinglondon.co.uk

Tennis

* Wimbledon Lawn Tennis Club

Day passes can be purchased during the championships for as little as £8 and resale tickets for matches start at a little as £10.
www.wimbledon.com

Sport

* Queen Elizabeth Olympic Park
London E15

The Olympic Park Stratford was London's very successful venue for the London 2012 Olympic Games. The site is now being transformed into a multi purpose venue for all to enjoy.
www.queenelizabetholympicpark.co.uk

* FREE Events
FREE events include classes, festivals, workshops and more.
See website for details:

Storytelling

* Discover Children's Storytelling Centre London E15
London's only children's museum is a place where children and their families can enjoy playing, learning and making up stories together.
Concession £4 Adult £4.50
www.discover.org.uk

Thrifty Tip
Discover Children's Storytelling Centre Journey to Space Interactive Family Exhibition
Children and their families are given a vital mission to find missing astronaut Major Tom.
www.discover.org.uk

Horniman Museum London SE23
During AUG/SEPT their popular storytellers bring their collections and gardens alive with enchanting stories from around the world.
www.horniman.ac.uk

Quirky London

* Camden Beach Roundhouse
London NW1

Camden Beach at the Roundhouse is 900 square metres and 150 tonnes of the finest sand, with end-of-the-pier amusements, deckchairs, beach huts, ice creams,ping pong, live music, and loads more. If you can't get to the beach, the Roundhouse is bringing the beach to you.
FREE Annual Event
See website
www.roundhouse.org.uk

Carnaby Street
London W1

Carnaby Street in the 60s proved popular for followers of both the Mod and hippie styles. Many independent fashion boutiques and designers such as Mary Quant, Lord John, Take Six, and Irvine Sellars were located in Carnaby Street. It is still a popular destination in London today.
www.carnaby.co.uk

.

Interesting Fact
Carnaby Street

Bands such as the Small Faces, The Who, and Rolling Stones all appearing in the nearby Marquee Club.

Signal Box Visits
St Albans
Hertfordshire
As part of the Heritage Open Days St Albans Signal box opens it's doors to the public. They run signalling demonstrations on the operating floor. Light refreshments available.
Admission FREE
www.tlr.ltd.uk/sigbox/opendays.eb

London's Oldest Coaching Inn

The George Inn
Sourhwark SE1
Currently owned and leased by the National Trust It is Londons only surviving galleried coaching Inn.
www.nationaltrust.org.uk/george-inn

London's Smallest Pub

The Dove
London W6
Sitting next to the fire, or out on the Dove's riverside terrace, you are not just sitting in any old local you are a part of London's rich history. The small space to the right of the bar, reached through an extra entrance went into the Guinness Book of World Records as the smallest bar room in the world.
www.dovehammersmith.co.uk

Acknowledgements

With grateful thanks to all our family and friends, without your continued support this Guide book would not have been possible (we love you all). Special thanks to Maria & Mike Trish for typing and proof reading.

Big thanks to Louise Collarbon for the amazing cover design, and to Steve Lowy Umi Hotels London for the Inspiration.

Big thanks also to our Special family member in London for all the thrifty London knowledge she has passed on to us over the years (you know who you are!).

Disclaimer:
All details contained in this guide where correct
at time of going to print. Please check
individual websites for latest details and listings.

Printed in Great Britain
by Amazon.co.uk, Ltd.,
Marston Gate.